AMERICAN NEUTRALITY

1914–1917

ESSAYS ON THE
CAUSES OF AMERICAN INTERVENTION
IN THE WORLD WAR

BY

CHARLES SEYMOUR

NEW HAVEN · YALE UNIVERSITY PRESS

LONDON · HUMPHREY MILFORD · OXFORD UNIVERSITY PRESS

1935

CONTENTS

INTRODUCTION

How can the United States stay out of the next European war? The question has received more widespread attention during the past few months than at any other time in our history. This is partly due to the lowering clouds of war overseas, partly to America's increasing appreciation of the futility and the cost of war as an instrument of national policy. Nothing is more certain than the intense determination of the people of the United States that the surest way to peace must be discovered.

It is natural and wise that in this search the conditions that brought us into the last war should be studied. It may be that from such study we can learn how to avoid entanglement in other wars. As Patrick Henry insisted, there is no lamp for the path of the future except the experience of the past. Unfortunately, history is not an exact science and it is easy to expound it in simple but inaccurate terms. There is always the temptation to lay the blame for misfortunes of the past upon single individuals or special groups, and sometimes to impute to them motives of a low order. Thus United States Senators, conducting an official investigation, have not hesitated to aver that we entered the war "to save the skins of bankers," or because of the trade of a small group of munitions makers, and that even the President of the United States was not honest in the picture he gave to the country of the causes that compelled American intervention.

Such generalizations are quite unfair to the statesmen and business leaders of the past. They are dangerous if they are utilized as a basis for the policy of the future. Any program starting from unhistorical grounds is sure to be unrealistic. If legislative measures can be taken in time of peace to keep us at peace when other nations are at war, they must be drafted in accord with the experience of the past accurately understood. It is at least questionable whether there is any type of realistic legislation that will serve to keep us at peace if our important interests are attacked; we may reach the conclusion that the only means of avoiding intervention in another European war is to assist in preventing that war.

But in order to answer the question and to ponder the conclusion, it is essential that the facts and not the fiction of our entrance into the last war should be taken as the point of departure.

The brief essays that follow are designed to correct a number of mistaken explanations of our intervention in the European war in April, 1917. They revolve mainly around the figure of President Wilson, because of his control of foreign relations. They do not by any means constitute a comprehensive survey of all the problems of neutrality. So far as they go, however, they are based upon the original documentary sources. It is from such sources rather than from hasty opinion that a program of future peace should be derived.

C. S.

Yale University,
  November 5, 1935.

AMERICAN NEUTRALITY

I

AMERICAN NEUTRALITY[1]

THE EXPERIENCE OF 1914–17

RECENT discussions of the causes of American intervention in the World War have stirred emotions; but they have failed to suggest conclusively measures that might have served to keep us at peace. There is talk of the intrigues of munitions makers and the greed of capitalists. Less fantastic is the revival of the thesis that if we had treated Germany and the Allies with an even hand in meeting their attacks upon American neutral rights, we might have avoided intervention. A popular outline of the years 1914–17, by Mr. Walter Millis, implies that as we had permitted infractions of our rights by the Allies we had no right to protest to the point of war against Germany's use of the submarine. But he suggests no practicable alternatives to the policy followed by President Wilson. The country slithered into war,

1. Reprinted by permission from *Foreign Affairs,* October, 1935.

he evidently feels, much as Lloyd George once remarked that Europe had slithered into war in 1914. "Among them all," Mr. Millis writes of the Americans of 1917, "none quite knew how it had happened, nor why. . . ."

There was at least one American who was acutely aware of why the United States was brought into the World War. This was the President of the United States, who for nearly three years struggled to maintain neutrality in the face of difficulties that finally proved uncontrollable. Whether as a basis for future policy, or merely to set the historical record straight, it is worth while to review Woodrow Wilson's fight to avoid intervention.

Any inquiry into the causes of American participation in the war must begin with the personality of Wilson. His office conferred upon him a determining influence in foreign policy which was heightened by the troubled state of affairs abroad. His character was such that he never let this influence slip into other hands. He was his own foreign secretary. Conscious of the power and character of public opinion, "under bonds," as he put it, to public sentiment, he nevertheless made the major decisions on his own responsibility. He delivered his "too proud to fight" speech and he sent Bernstorff home without stopping to ask what the man in the street would say. Dominant sentiment in the United States was certainly pro-Ally. American economic prosperity, furthermore, depended upon the maintenance of our trade with the Allies. But it is a far cry from these facts to the assumption that because of them we adopted a policy that pointed toward intervention. It would be necessary to show that emotional sympathy and material interests overcame the strong pacifistic sentiment of Congress and people. It would especially be necessary to show that because of them Wilson first adopted a discriminatory attitude toward Germany and then surrendered his determination to keep the country out of war.

Ample evidence is now available regarding Wilson's sentiments toward the belligerents. If it reveals an underlying personal sympathy with the Allies, it also reveals a studied insistence not to permit that feeling to affect national policy. He was so far successful that he was attacked in turn by each belligerent group as being favorable to the other. There can be no question that he regarded the maintenance of peace as his first duty. Always he held to the double principle he formulated at the moment he was smarting under the news of the *Arabic's* sinking in August, 1915: "1. The people of this country count on me to keep them out of the war; 2. It would be a calamity to the world at large if we should be actively drawn into the conflict and so deprived of all disinterested influence over the settlement." He maintained this attitude in the face of what he regarded as gross affronts by Germany. "The country is undoubtedly back of me in the whole matter," he wrote privately in September, 1915, "and I feel myself under bonds to it to show patience to the utmost. My chief puzzle is to determine where patience ceases to be a virtue."[2]

But across the determination to preserve peace ran the equally strong determination to preserve the neutral rights of the country.

2. Wilson to House, August 21, September 20, 1915, Charles Seymour, *American Diplomacy during the World War* (Baltimore, Johns Hopkins Press, 1934), pp. 101, 103–104. Hereafter cited as *Amer. Dipl.*

There was a higher principle which the President placed above peace: the honor of the United States. The outcome of this contradiction would be determined not by Wilson's policy but by that of the belligerents. He said in January, 1916:

I know that you are depending upon me to keep this Nation out of the war. So far I have done so and I pledge you my word that, God helping me, I will—if it is possible. But you have laid another duty upon me. You have bidden me see to it that nothing stains or impairs the honor of the United States, and that is a matter not within my control; that depends upon what others do, not upon what the Government of the United States does. Therefore there may at any moment come a time when I cannot preserve both the honor and the peace of the United States. Do not exact of me an impossible and contradictory thing.[3]

Against both groups of belligerents Wilson steadily maintained American neutral rights. It is by no means a fact that he accepted British and Allied infractions of what he described as "hitherto fixed international

3. Speech at Milwaukee, January 31, 1916, Ray Stannard Baker and William Edward Dodd, edd., *The Public Papers of Woodrow Wilson* (New York, Harper, 1925–27; 6 vols.), II, 48.

law." The notes of protest which he sponsored and which so greatly annoyed those who, like Ambassador Page, frankly favored the Allied cause, made clear that the United States did not, and would not, recognize the legality of the Allied pseudo-blockade. In the late summer of 1916 the President secured from Congress wide powers permitting him to prohibit loans and to impose embargoes if retaliatory measures appeared advisable. A few weeks later he asked House to warn Sir Edward Grey "in the strongest terms" that the American people were "growing more and more impatient with the intolerable conditions of neutrality, their feeling as hot against Great Britain as it was first against Germany. . . ."[4]

That he did not actually exercise the pressure of embargoes against the British and French resulted from two factors. The first was that the conflict over Allied interference with neutral trade was pushed into the background at critical moments by the more immediate and intense conflict with Germany over the submarine campaign. "If Germany

4. Wilson to House, November 24, 1916, Seymour, *Amer. Dipl.*, p. 79.

had not alienated American sympathies," wrote Colonel House, "by her mode of warfare, the United States would not have put up with Allied control of American trade on the high seas." The fact has been emphasized by Winston Churchill: "The first German U-boat campaign," he writes, "gave us our greatest assistance. It altered the whole position of our controversies with America. A great relief became immediately apparent."[5]

The second reason for not pushing the diplomatic conflict with the Allies to the point of retaliatory measures lay in the economic interests of America. Any practicable measures designed to enforce our interpretation of international law would have ruined the interests they meant to safeguard. By our formal protests we protected our ultimate property rights and built up a case for future damages to be proved before an international tribunal. Through private negotiations we secured in large measure the protection of immediate commercial interests. Whatever the inconvenience and delays

5. Winston Spencer Churchill, *The World Crisis, 1911–1918* (New York, Scribner, 1923–27; 4 vols.), II, 306.

experienced in our trade with the northern
European neutrals, American foreign commerce was deriving rich profits. Allied command of the sea did not touch our pockets so
much as our pride. As Ambassador Spring
Rice cabled to Grey, it seemed "objection-
able not because it is what it is, but because
it is so all-pervading."[6] Thus, if Wilson had
destroyed the basis of our prosperity in order to compel immediate acceptance of the
American interpretation of international
law, which very few Americans understood
and which even now is not entirely clear, he
would have provoked something like a revolt
against his administration. "If it came to the
last analysis," wrote House to Wilson in the
summer of 1915, "and we placed an embargo upon munitions of war and foodstuffs
to please the cotton men, our whole industrial and agricultural machinery would cry
out against it."[7] Wilson's policy was designed not to favor the Allies but to protect

6. Stephen Gwynn, ed., *The Letters and Friendships of Sir
Cecil Spring Rice* (Boston, Houghton Mifflin, 1929; 2 vols.),
II, 243.

7. July 22, 1915, Seymour, *The Intimate Papers of Colonel
House* (Boston, Houghton Mifflin, 1926, 1928; 4 vols.), II,
58. Hereafter cited as *I.P.*

the immediate interests of the nation and at the same time to preserve our ultimate legal rights. He yielded no principle and surrendered no claim.

The German attack upon American rights Wilson believed to be of an entirely different nature and one that must be met by different methods. The intensive submarine campaign was the answer to the system of Allied maritime control; logically, an excuse might be found for it. But its effects upon neutral rights were far more disastrous. For technical reasons and to operate effectively, the submarines must make their attack without warning, destroy blindly, escape as speedily as possible, leaving the sinking merchant ship, which might be neutral or belligerent, which might or might not carry contraband, with no assurance of what would happen to passengers and crew. To Wilson and to dominant American opinion, such wholesale methods of destroying enemy and neutral commerce were shocking. This was no question of "juridical niceties." The submarine campaign, unlike the Allied blockade, involved undiscriminating destruction of American property rights. It permitted no distinction between contraband and free goods. The Allied system gave to the American shipper reasonable assurance of safe passage after he had complied with certain formalities. Under the threat of the submarine the shipper faced the risk of losing his entire cargo. The Allied system did not involve the loss of American ships; if held in a British prize court the owner could find protection for them in legal procedure. The German submarine threatened the loss of the ship and the death of crew and passengers as well.

Thus, from the point of view of material interests, there could be no comparison between the damage resulting to Americans from the Allied blockade and that from the intensive submarine campaign. If the latter were permitted, under protests comparable to those sent to the Allies, the result would be an almost complete blockade of American commerce, since shippers would not dare send cargoes and crew out to destruction. A clear illustration of the effect of the submarine campaign on American commercial, industrial, and agricultural interests was given by the congestion of our ports that followed the threat of submarine attacks in February and March, 1917. Freights were snarled, goods were spoiled, business was menaced with a complete tie-up.

Even so, Wilson might not have taken his firm stand against the submarine if merely property rights had been threatened. He was always careful not to interpret national policy in terms of purely material interests. Despite the difficulties involved, the economic aspects of the diplomatic conflict with Germany might have been adjudicated. But the submarine warfare involved attacks upon American lives, whether sailors on merchant ships or passengers. To Wilson it seemed a war on humanity. Between property interests and human rights there lay a clear distinction. It was brought home to all America when, on May 7, 1915, the *Lusitania* was sunk without warning, over eleven hundred persons drowned, men, women, and children, among them more than one hundred and twenty Americans. Wilson wrote:

The sinking of passenger ships involves principles of humanity which throw into the background any special circumstances of detail that may be thought to affect the cases, principles which lift it, as the Imperial German Government will no doubt be quick to recognize and acknowledge, out of the class of ordinary subjects of diplomatic discussion or of international controversy. . . . The Government of the United States is contending for something much greater than mere rights of property or privileges of commerce. It is contending for nothing less high and sacred than the rights of humanity, which every Government honors itself in respecting and no Government is justified in resigning on behalf of those under its care and authority.[8]

It has been frequently suggested that since the submarine campaign was designed to interrupt the flow of munitions from the United States to the Allies, Wilson might have imposed embargoes upon the export of munitions as a diplomatic bribe to Germany to give up the intensive use of the submarine. There is no indication that the President ever seriously considered this course. He was willing to utilize embargoes, if necessary as measures of retaliation against the Allies in the defense of American rights. But

8. Note of June 9, 1915, U.S. Department of State, *Papers relating to the Foreign Relations of the United States,* Supplement. *The World War:* 1915, pp. 436–438. (Edited by Tyler Dennett and Joseph V. Fuller. Washington, Government Printing Office, 1928.) Hereafter cited as *F.R.*

he was not willing to penalize ourselves in order to redress the inherent disadvantage of Germany resulting from Allied command of the seas. He agreed with Lansing that such a policy ran counter to the neutral duties of the United States. It would certainly have ruined not merely the "war babies" of industry, but the cotton and wheat growers, the copper producers, the iron and steel workers, and have thrown the country back into the bleak depression and unemployment from which it had just emerged.

There is no evidence that even the broadest sort of American embargo would have induced the Germans to forego the intensive use of the submarine. They meant to stop British imports of all raw materials, especially foodstuffs, not merely from the United States but from South America, India, and the Dominions. The purpose of the submarine campaign was far wider than the interruption of the Allied "munitions" trade with America; it was, according to the testimony given to the Reichstag investigating committee, designed to throw over the British the deadly fear of complete starvation and thus to compel them to sue for peace on German terms. Hindenburg and Ludendorff made quite plain that, in the winter of 1916–17, nothing but the prospect of immediate peace on such terms could have prevented the resumption of the submarine campaign.[9]

Wilson, of course, might have avoided a break with Germany by surrendering the right to send American ships and citizens out on the high seas. Thus they would not be sunk by submarines. Such a policy was suggested by Mr. Bryan and was later embodied in the Gore-McLemore resolutions brought before Congress. The President believed that no government was justified in making this surrender. Through his protests to the Allies he had secured, without yielding any principle, a working arrangement that gave reasonable protection to American commercial interests. Now if, under the threat of the German submarine, he withdrew protection on the seas from American goods, sailors, and passengers, he would sacrifice interests that no protests could compensate and yield principles that noth-

9. See *infra*, pp. 78–80.

ing in the future could make good. He wrote
to Senator Stone:

No nation, no group of nations, has the right,
while war is in progress, to alter or disregard the
principles which all nations have agreed upon in
mitigation of the horrors and sufferings of war;
and if the clear rights of American citizens
should ever unhappily be abridged or denied by
such action, we should, it seems to me, have in
honor no choice as to what our own course
should be. . . . We covet peace and shall preserve it at any cost but the loss of honor. To forbid our people to exercise their rights for fear
we might be called upon to vindicate them would
be a deep humiliation indeed.

It was all very well, Wilson pointed out,
to argue that the material value of these
rights could not be compared with the cost
of a war. But if you begin to surrender accepted rights, where do you stop?

If in this instance we allowed expediency to take
the place of principle, the door would inevitably
be opened to still further concessions. Once accept a single abatement of right, and many other
humiliations would certainly follow. . . . What
we are contending for in this matter is of the
very essence of the things that have made
America a sovereign nation. She cannot yield

them without conceding her own impotency as a Nation and making virtual surrender of her independent position among the nations of the world.[10]

Such was Wilson's position, written for all the world and especially for Germany to read. He maintained it consistently from the first declaration of submarine warfare in February, 1915, two years before the final break, when he warned the German Government that it would be held to "a strict accountability" for acts endangering American lives and property, and that the American Government would take any necessary steps to "secure to American citizens the full enjoyment of their acknowledged rights on the high seas." This warning was translated into specific terms a year later, after the sinking of the *Sussex*, taking the form of an ultimatum which left no further room for negotiation:

Unless the Imperial Government should now immediately declare and effect an abandonment of its present methods of submarine warfare against passenger and freight-carrying vessels, the Government of the United States can have

10. *F.R.*, 1916, Supp., pp. 177–178.

no choice but to sever diplomatic relations with the German Empire altogether.[11]

The Germans yielded, if only for the moment, as a result of this definite warning. During the course of 1915 they had taken Von Bernstorff's warnings not too seriously, and heeded them largely because they had not yet themselves realized what a powerful weapon they possessed in the submarine. After Wilson's *Sussex* note they were under no illusions. "There was no longer any doubt in Berlin," wrote the German Ambassador, "that persistence in the point of view they had hitherto adopted would bring about a break with the United States." But in the early autumn Hindenburg and Ludendorff threw their influence in favor of a resumption of the submarine campaign. The discussions in Berlin were clearly based upon the assumption of war with the United States. Bethmann-Hollweg later testified before the Reichstag committee:

The U-boat war meant a break and, later, war with America. It was on this point that for years the argument between the military and the po-

11. Note of April 18, 1916, *F.R.*, 1916, Supp., pp. 232–234.

litical branch had turned. The decisive point was that the Supreme High Command of the Army from now on was absolutely determined to assume the responsibility of the risk which an American war meant. . . .[12]

The one chance of preventing the resumption of the submarine campaign, and thus keeping the United States out of war, lay in peace negotiations. Bernstorff judged correctly that neither Wilson nor public opinion would permit America to enter the war on any issue other than the submarine, and that it was vital to secure a postponement of the intensive campaign. He telegraphed to von Jagow, July 13, 1916:

If it once comes to peace negotiations between the combatants, I regard it as out of the question—even were they to fail—that the United States would enter the war against us. American public feeling in favor of peace is too strong for that. It required the hysterical excitement roused by the *Lusitania* question, and the incidents connected with it, to produce a state of mind among Americans which at times made war seem inevitable. In the absence of similar

12. Carnegie Endowment for International Peace, Division of International Law. *Official German Documents relating to the World War* (New York, Oxford University Press, 1925; 2 vols.), I, 344. Hereafter cited as *G.D.*

incidents, such a state of feeling could not be aroused.[18]

Hence the eagerness with which he pressed upon Colonel House the importance of peace action by Wilson before it was too late. Hence also the determination with which Wilson, who realized the approaching danger, prepared his peace note of December 18, 1916. He wanted to make it, he wrote House, "the strongest and most convincing thing I ever penned."

In the circumstances the effort was bound to fail. Its effect was confused by the issuance of Bethmann's peace statement on December 12, which made Wilson's note appear to the Allies as part of a plan to rescue the Central Powers from defeat. The Allies were quite unwilling to negotiate with an unbeaten Germany. The Germans were determined to insist upon terms which the Allies would not have accepted until all hope of victory had faded. Neither side wished the mediation of Wilson. The British, according to Sir William Wiseman, felt that Wilson merely talked about ideals for which the Al-

13. Count Johann Heinreich Bernstorff, *My Three Years in America* (New York, Scribner, 1920), pp. 280–281.

lies were dying. "We entertain but little hope," von Jagow had written to Bernstorff, "for the result of the exercise of good offices by one whose instincts are all in favor of the English point of view, and who in addition to this, is so naïve a statesman as President Wilson." The new German Foreign Secretary, Zimmermann, said to the budget committee of the Reichstag: "The good thing about the break with the United States is that we have finally gotten rid of this person as peace mediator."[14]

Wilson was not discouraged by the failure of the December peace notes. He worked all through January to secure a private statement of German terms, equipped with which he could start negotiations with the Allies. He was determined to save American neutrality. On January 4, 1917, in reply to House's suggestion of the need of military preparation "in the event of war," the President insisted: "There will be no war. This country does not intend to become involved in this war. We are the only one of the great white nations that is free from war today,

14. *G.D.*, II, 977–978, 409.

and it would be a crime against civilization for us to go in."[15] On January 22 he delivered before the Senate the address which he hoped would serve as a general basis for a negotiated peace, a settlement that would leave neither the one side nor the other crushed and revengeful, "a peace without victory." It opened, as British writers later insisted, the "last opportunity of ending the war with a real peace. For America was still pacific and impartial. . . . But unhappily for mankind, the British and Prussian war machines had by then taken charge."

It is possible that if Germany had then held her hand Wilson might have been able to force negotiations. The Allies were beginning to scrape the bottom of the money chest and the time was approaching when they would be dependent upon American credits. He could soon have exercised strong pressure upon them. On the other side the Kaiser, Bethmann, and Bernstorff had no profound confidence in the submarine and were inclined toward compromise. But the decision had already been taken in Ger-

15. *I.P.*, II, 412.

many. On January 9 Hindenburg and Holt-
zendorf insisted that all chance of peace had
disappeared and forced approval of the intensive submarine campaign. On January 31
Bernstorff gave notice that from the following day the engagements of the pledge given
after the sinking of the *Sussex* would no
longer be observed.

Thus ended Wilson's last effort to achieve
a compromise peace, and the rupture between Germany and the United States became inevitable. The President saw no escape from the fulfilment of the warning he
had given the previous April. The shock was
the worse for Wilson inasmuch as it came
just as he hoped to initiate mediation. He
said "he felt as if the world had suddenly re-
versed itself; that after going from east to
west, it had begun to go from west to east
and he could not get his balance."[16] Resentment against Germany, with whom he had
been working for peace, was strong. He felt
with House that Germany "desires some
justification for her submarine warfare and
thought she could get it by declaring her

16. *I.P.*, II, 439–441.

willingness to make peace." Bernstorff himself insists that it was the German declaration of submarine warfare and nothing else
that mattered with Wilson.

From that time henceforward—there can be no
question of any earlier period, because up to
that time he had been in constant negotiation
with us—he regarded the Imperial Government
as morally condemned. . . . After January 31,
1917, Wilson himself was a different man. Our
rejection of his proposal to mediate, by our an-
nouncement of the unrestricted U-boat war,
which was to him utterly incomprehensible,
turned him into an embittered enemy of the Imperial Government.[17]

Even after the diplomatic rupture Wilson
waited long weeks, to give every opportunity
to the Germans to avoid war. Only actual
overt acts would persuade him that they
would carry their policy into effect. He was
willing to negotiate everything except the
sinking of passenger and merchant ships
without warning. The Germans showed no
sign of weakening. When it was suggested
that America might be kept neutral if the
submarines "overlooked" American boats,

17. Bernstorff, *op. cit.*, p. 385.

the Kaiser wrote on the margin of the memorandum which disapproved the suggestion
on technical grounds: "Agreed, reject. . . .
Now, once for all, an *end* to negotiations
with America. If Wilson wants war, let him
make it, and let him then have it."[18] On
March 27, following the sinking of four
American ships, the President took the decision, and on April 2 he asked Congress to declare the existence of a state of war with
Germany.

So far as tests can be applied, Wilson's position was approved by the American people.
Like him they were determined to stay at
peace so far as the exercise of their acknowledged rights could keep them at peace, but
they regarded the submarine attacks as acts
of war. They were by no means prepared to
sacrifice American rights on the seas and
adopt a policy of nonintercourse with European belligerents and neutrals which would
have resulted in economic depression or
disaster in the United States. So much is
indicated by the votes in Congress on the
Gore-McLemore resolutions and the armed

18. *G.D.*, II, 1336.

shipping bill which gave overwhelming en-
dorsement to Wilson's policy. On the other
hand, whatever the emotional sympathy for
the Allied cause in the United States and
however close Allied and American commercial interests, the prevailing sentiment of the
people was indelibly for peace until the submarines sank American ships. They re-
warded the patience with which Wilson carried on long negotiations over the *Lusitania*
as well as the firmness with which he issued
the *Sussex* ultimatum by reëlecting him
President in the autumn of 1916. He owed
his victory to the pacifists. So far from being
accused of chauvinism because of the stand
he had taken against the submarine campaign, he was presented and elected on the
basis of having "kept us out of war." But
when on April 2, following the destruction of
American ships, he declared that peace was
no longer consistent with honor, Congress
voted for war by tremendous majorities.

It frequently happens that the occasion
for an event is mistaken for its cause. Sometimes, however, the occasion and the cause
are the same. There is every evidence that

the sole factor that could have driven Wilson from neutrality in the spring of 1917 was the resumption of the submarine campaign. On the very eve of his war speech he was seized by his hunger for peace.

For nights, he said, he'd been lying awake over the whole situation. . . . He said he couldn't see any alternative, that he had tried every way he knew to avoid war . . . had considered every loophole of escape, and as fast as they were discovered Germany deliberately blocked them with some new outrage.[19]

In the circumstances there was no escape, for the point had been reached which he had long foreseen and dreaded, where he could not preserve both the peace and honor of the United States. "There is one choice we cannot make, we are incapable of making," he told Congress on April 2. "We will not choose the path of submission."

19. John L. Heaton, *Cobb of "The World"* (New York, Dutton, 1924), pp. 268–270.

II

WOODROW WILSON AND THE
SUBMARINE CAMPAIGN

IT is not uninteresting to note how frequently discussion of the causes of American
intervention in the World War proceeds
without any reference to President Wilson,
who made the final decision, and without
any reference to the German submarine
campaign, which occasioned that decision.
As we have observed, stress is laid on the influence of munitions makers, who are supposed first to have fathered the preparedness
movement and then favored participation in
the war. Stress is also laid upon the Allied
connections of the bankers and their anxiety
to protect loans that were supposed to be en-
dangered by Allied defeat. But no effective
attempt has been made to show that either
munitions makers or bankers exercised any
influence upon Congress, which voted the
war resolution, or upon the President, who
asked for it.

Wilson himself has answered the charge
that the preparedness movement was incited

by the munitions makers; his answer would
serve equally to apply to their alleged influence in pushing us into war. On February 1,
1916, speaking at Des Moines on the need of
military preparations, he said:

I have heard the preposterous statement made
that the agitation for preparation for national
defense has come chiefly from the men who
make armor plate for the ships and munitions
for the Army. Why, ladies and gentlemen, do
you suppose that all the thoughtful men who are
engaged upon this side of this great question are
susceptible of being led by influences of that
sort? . . . I have not found the impulse for national defense coming from those sources. . . .
I found it coming from the men who have nothing to do with the making of profits, but who
have everything to do with the making of the
daily life of this country. And it is from them
that I take my inspiration. . . . Of course some-
body is going to make money out of the things
privately manufactured, manufactured by private capital. There are men now in the great
belligerent countries making, I dare say, vast
sums of money out of the war, but making it perfectly legitimately, and I for one do not stand
here to challenge or doubt their patriotism in the
matter.[1]

1. Text of speech in Baker and Dodd, edd., *op. cit.*, II,
70–82.

As to the charge that the policy of the United States was influenced by the bankers, the President may have heard it, for it was raised on various occasions on the floor of Congress during the debates of March, 1917, but he never bothered to answer it. Nor has it ever been seriously considered by historians. The whole trend of the reform legislation of 1913–14 was directed against the control of affairs by concentrated capital. The President himself was careful to avoid personal contact with the representatives of capitalist interests and by temperament and association was almost the last person in the country to be influenced by them. So much is indicated by his public and private papers. If we are seeking an explanation of Wilson's willingness to yield his determined pacifism, in 1917, and ask for a declaration of war, the search must be made, not among domestic influences and certainly not among influences of a material kind, but rather in the impact of foreign factors. Of these, the one of greatest importance, perhaps the only one of importance, was the German submarine campaign.

During the first six months of the war offi-

cial relations between the United States and
Germany were not disturbed by any serious
difficulty. Wilson himself, although tem-
peramentally and by inheritance inclined to
favor the cause of the Allies, was determined
that there should be no official hint of his
personal feeling; and even on the personal
side he was irritated by the trade restrictions
of the Allies. From German individuals
there came strong complaint of the export
from America of munitions of war, which because of their command of the seas went
almost exclusively to Great Britain and
France. But the German Government was
not in a position to protest such exports. Indeed, Ambassador Bernstorff, at a moment
when Germany was striving to procure supplies for her warships still operating on the
high seas, quoted with approval the State
Department memorandum of August 15
which emphasized the right to sell munitions, and frankly conceded the legitimacy
of American trade in contraband with the
Allies. He admitted:

Under the general principles of international
law, no exception can be taken to neutral states

letting war material go to Germany's enemies
from or through their territory. This is in accordance with Article 7 of the Hague conven-
tions of October 18, 1907, concerning the rights
and duties of neutrals in naval and land war.[2]

This concession was not surprising. Germany herself had profited by trade with belligerents in previous wars. Germany and
Austria had sold supplies to Great Britain
during the Boer War, in circumstances
which bore close analogy with those of the
World War, since the Boers at the time were
cut off by the British from access to the German market. Germany and Austria had sold
munitions to the belligerents in the Russo-
Japanese War, in the Italo-Turkish War of
1911, and in both the Balkan Wars of the
next two years.[3]

But the relative placidity of relations between the United States and Germany was
shattered on February 4, 1915, by the German declaration making the territorial wa-
ters of Great Britain and Ireland, including
the English Channel, a war zone. Germany
gave warning that from February 18 onward

2. *F.R.*, 1914, Supp., p. 647.
3. *F.R.*, 1915, Supp., pp. 788–789.

every merchant ship encountered in this
area was liable to be sunk; neutral shipping,
it was declared, was liable to the same dan-
gers; the safety of passengers and crews
could not be promised.[4] Germany took as
justification for this declaration, which by
implication was admittedly contrary to the
custom of nations, the earlier declaration by
the British of November 2, 1914, proclaiming the North Sea a war zone, and also the
seizure of foodstuffs destined for Germany's
civilian population. It was thus an act of reprisal against Allied methods of blockade.
The war zone was also designed to interrupt
the import of munitions into Great Britain
and France.

President Wilson without delay laid down
the policy to which he held without devia-
tion for two years. Acts of reprisal, contrary
to international law, if they attacked Ameri-

4. *F.R.,* 1915, Supp., pp. 94, 96–97; Grand Admiral Alfred
von Tirpitz, *My Memoirs* (London, Hurst and Blackett,
1929; 2 vols.), II, 390–399.

On the development of German submarine policy, see
Adolphe Laurens, *Histoire de la guerre sous-marine alle-
mande.* Also, the testimony of Bethmann, Zimmermann, Von
Capelle, and Admiral Koch before the Reichstag Investigating Committee, published in *G.D.*

can rights and lives could not be admitted. The American note of February 10 read:

If the commanders of German vessels should . . . destroy on the high seas an American vessel or the lives of American citizens, it would be difficult for the Government of the United States to view the act in any other light than as an indefensible violation of neutral rights. . . . The Government of the United States would be constrained to hold the Imperial German Government to a strict accountability for such acts of their naval authorities and to take any steps it might be necessary to take to safeguard American lives and property and to secure to American citizens the full enjoyment of their acknowledged rights on the high seas.

Thus, two full years before American intervention in the war, Germany received clear notice that American lives and property would be protected by any steps "it might be necessary to take."[5]

Wilson followed up this definite warning with the suggestion to the belligerents that each side give up its illegal weapons, the Allies their methods of blockade, the Germans

5. Lansing to Gerard, February 15, 1915, *F.R.*, 1915, Supp., pp. 98–100.

their submarine. The Allies at first refused; later Grey intimated that if the Germans would give up the illegal use of the submarine and the use of poison gas, the British would permit foodstuffs to enter Germany. But this the Germans refused, revealing thereby that the so-called "hunger-blockade" was not a determining factor. They would give up the submarine only if raw materials as well were admitted.[6] For they intended by this weapon to break the Allied blockade completely.

The Germans were slow to realize the capability of the submarine as a weapon offsetting Allied surface command of the seas. They possessed an insufficient number and those they had lacked extensive cruising range. Thus the early stages of the intensive campaign against merchant shipping did comparatively little harm to the Allies. But the campaign early brought the issue with the United States to a head. In March an American citizen was drowned when the *Falaba* was sunk; on May 1 the *Gulflight*,

6. Gerard to House, May 24, 1915, *I.P.*, I, 448. The German Foreign Minister told Gerard that Germany was in no need of food.

an American oilboat, was sunk with the loss of two lives; on May 7 the *Lusitania* was sunk with the loss of over a thousand.

The sinking of the *Lusitania* had consequences from which German diplomacy never recovered. As Ambassador von Bernstorff admits, it was thereafter impossible to arouse sympathy for the cause of Germany in the United States; all that could be done was to keep the United States out of the war. How near we were then and in the ensuing weeks to actual war, his letters and memoirs make clear. Had Wilson chosen to make the drowning of American citizens at that time a *casus belli,* he would, according to Bernstorff, "have had American public opinion more decidedly behind him than it was later, at the time of the final breach. Not a voice would have been raised in opposition, except that of the Secretary of State, Mr. Bryan."[7] So great was the storm of emotion aroused.

Wilson, however, was determined that the United States should not be drawn into the war by any emotional factors, and he believed it possible by the exercise of patience

7. Bernstorff, *op. cit.,* p. 151.

and firmness to persuade Germany to give
up submarine attacks without warning upon
merchant shipping. At bottom the United
States, he knew, was strongly pacifistic. This
conviction strengthened his determination
to maintain unbreakable patience in the
midst of the popular uproar on the eastern
seaboard for strong action against Germany.
But he admitted to House that a point might
come where patience would cease "to be a
virtue."[8]

This patience he continued to display
even after the sinking of the *Arabic* in late
August, in the midst of his negotiations with
Germany over the *Lusitania*. But he was
equally determined that Germany should
yield on the main issue and that there should
be no evasion. He brushed aside what he regarded as technicalities in the German argument for the right to sink without warning.
He wrote in his note of June 9:

The sinking of passenger ships involves principles of humanity which throw into the background any special circumstances of detail. . . .
The Government of the United States is con-

8. Wilson to House, September 20, 1915, *Amer. Dipl.*, pp.
103–104.

tending for something much greater than mere
rights of property or privileges of commerce. It
is contending for nothing less high and sacred
than the rights of humanity, which every Government honors itself in respecting and which no
Government is justified in resigning on behalf
of those under its care and authority.[9]

It was argued in certain quarters in Germany that Wilson's patience was stronger
than his firmness and that there was no need
to bother about his susceptibilities. A good
many felt that America could do little to
injure German chances of victory. House
wrote to Wilson on June 16:

Tirpitz will continue his submarine policy, leaving the Foreign Office to make explanations for
any "unfortunate incidents" as best they may.
I think that we shall find ourselves drifting into
war with Germany, for there is a large element
in the German naval and military factions that
consider it would be a good, rather than a bad,
thing for Germany.[10]

Ambassador Gerard reported from Berlin:

It is the German hope to keep the *Lusitania*
matter "jollied along" until the American people
get excited about baseball or a new scandal and

9. *F.R.*, 1915, Supp., pp. 436–438.   10. *I.P.*, I, 469.

forget. Meantime the hate of America grows daily.[11]

Ambassador von Bernstorff, however, warned Berlin that Wilson was serious and the Kaiser, without making them public, gave orders that liners should not be sunk without warning and without provisions for the safety of crew and passengers. After the sinking of the *Arabic*, on August 19, and the loss of two American lives, the two nations, according to Bernstorff, approached the "brink of war." Only the publication by the German Ambassador of the orders not to sink without warning and a full disavowal of the commander of the submarine that sank the *Arabic* prevented a diplomatic rupture. Bernstorff telegraphed to Berlin:

From the date of the sinking of the *Lusitania,* America has always been on the verge of breaking off diplomatic relations with us. . . . By dint of drawing out the negotiations as long as possible, and by the employment of all my persuasive powers, I succeeded in tiding over the moment of *acute* tension. Then came the incident of the *Arabic*. My laboriously constructed diplomatic edifice came tumbling about my ears,

11. Gerard to House, June 1, 1915, *I.P.,* I, 454–455.

and things looked blacker than ever. . . . The only really important question as regards the settlement of the *Arabic* case, is whether it is worth while for us to risk a rupture of relations with the United States, for the sake of this affair. I still persist in my opinion, that it would infallibly have led us into a new war.[12]

German concessions and Wilson's patience led to a five-month lull in the submarine-warfare crisis. But the German Foreign Office had to meet an increasingly strong demand on the part of navy officials, supported by influential civilian opinion, for the unrestricted use of the submarine. This demand triumphed so far in February, 1916, that on the eighth of that month the German Government announced that, shortly, armed merchant vessels would be regarded as ships of war and treated accordingly. Thus began the so-called "sharpened submarine warfare." A new issue accordingly arose with Germany: whether defensive armament transformed a merchant vessel into a warship. But the issue was almost immediately overclouded by the crisis that re-

12. Bernstorff to German Foreign Office, October 20, 1915, *My Three Years in America*, pp. 192–194.

sulted from the sinking of the *Sussex,* on
March 24, 1916.

The *Sussex* was a Channel steamer, an un-
armed passenger boat, torpedoed without
warning. Eighty noncombatant passengers
were killed or wounded. American citizens
were on board but none of them lost their
lives. Secretary Lansing was in favor of an
immediate rupture with Germany; it was futile and humiliating, he believed, to drag out
more negotiations. Bernstorff warned his
Government that an immediate disavowal
was the only means of avoiding war. Everything depended upon the conflict in Berlin
between the advocates and opponents of the
submarine warfare. The German Ambassador wrote:

It was now a question of bend or break. I had no
means of knowing whether the supporters of the
submarine campaign or the partisans of an understanding with the United States would win
the day. In the former case war was inevitable.[13]

His opinion was justified by the note
which on April 18 Wilson sent to Germany:

Unless the Imperial Government should now

13. Bernstorff, *op. cit.,* p. 243.

immediately declare and effect an abandonment of its present methods of submarine warfare against passenger and freight-carrying vessels, the Government of the United States can have no choice but to sever diplomatic relations with the German Empire altogether.

This was an ultimatum which, if then or later disregarded by Germany, meant a rupture. Bernstorff wrote:

There was no longer any doubt in Berlin that persistence in the point of view they had hitherto adopted would bring about a break with the United States, for I received instructions to make all preparations for German merchant ships lying in American ports to be rendered useless by the destruction of their engines.[14]

The German Chancellor and the Foreign Secretary, striving hard for peace with America, met the determined opposition of the navy leaders, who had just embarked upon an extensive submarine construction program. The former triumphed. On May 4 a German note promised not to sink any merchant vessel, even within the war zone, without warning and rescue of the passen-

14. Bernstorff, *op. cit.*, p. 250.

gers and crew, unless they attempted to escape or offer resistance. It added, however, a qualifying paragraph to the effect that if the United States could not succeed in altering the Allied blockade, the German Government would consider themselves faced by a new situation, for which they must reserve for themselves full freedom of decision.[15]

Thus Germany yielded for the moment, under the threat of diplomatic rupture, but intimated that later, if unable to stand the Allied blockade they would resume the unrestricted submarine warfare. Public opinion in Germany resented America. "Every night," wrote Ambassador Gerard, "fifty million Germans cry themselves to sleep because all Mexico has not risen against us."[16] The German naval chiefs were embittered by the concessions of the political leaders, which ruined the effectiveness of the submarine just at the moment when it promised important results.[17]

Ambassador von Bernstorff was definite in his reports that a resumption of the un-

15. *F.R.*, 1916, Supp., pp. 257–260.
16. Gerard to House, April 5, 1916, *I.P.*, II, 246.
17. Andreas Heinrich Michelsen, *Der U-bootskrieg* (Leipzig, Koehler, 1925), pp. 58–59.

restricted warfare would bring the United States in; it was the only thing, in his opinion, that would. He hoped that the German Government would recognize the impossibility of victory and help Wilson in his efforts for peace mediation. Even if the negotiations failed, they would serve to convince America of the sincerity of German intentions and win the approval of American pacifist opinion. Popular feeling in America, he insisted, would not be turned into warlike channels unless another submarine crisis, with the accompanying "hysteria" should intervene.[18]

But the German Foreign Office was hard pressed by the advocates of the submarine, who insisted on attempts to combat Allied command of the seas. "The Army and Navy are again urging submarine warfare," telegraphed Von Jagow on June 12, "as the only weapon against England, and particularly against her blockade." He went on to ask whether Wilson would still press matters to war if human lives could be spared in the submarine campaign. Bernstorff was categoric in his warning.

18. Bernstorff, *op. cit.*, pp. 280–281.

Assuming that it is intended that the resumption of the submarine campaign be accompanied by the official or clandestine withdrawal of the concessions granted in our note of the 4th May, such a withdrawal or modification of our concessions would in my opinion lead to a rupture and America's entry into the war.[19]

The efforts of Bernstorff and the civil officials of the German Government to prevent the renewal of the submarine campaign were based upon the conviction that no effects of the submarine warfare could possibly compensate for the disadvantage of American entrance into the war. "The attainment of peace through unrestricted submarine war seems hopeless," telegraphed Bernstorff on September 8, "since the United States would inevitably be drawn into the war . . . and consequently the war would be prolonged."[20] But on August 30 their policy received a blow in the appointment of Hindenburg and Ludendorff to become Chief of the General Staff and Quartermaster-General, respectively. Henceforth the military command exercised increasing influence in the deter-

19. Bernstorff to Von Jagow, June 19, 1916, *My Three Years in America*, pp. 283–284.
20. Bernstorff, *op. cit.*, p. 288.

mination of policy, while the influence of the Chancellor diminished. The immediate attention of Hindenburg and Ludendorff was taken by the entrance of Rumania into the war; but once that danger was parried they decided that unless peace could be secured by negotiation within a brief period, "unrestricted submarine warfare was now the only means left to secure in any reasonable time a victorious end to the war."[21] They were supported by the representatives of the German people. On October 7, 1916, the main committee of the Reichstag voted to approve the unrestricted submarine campaign if ordered by the Supreme Command. The date was later described by Vice-Chancellor von Payer as that which "determined Germany's doom."[22]

The one chance of the opponents of the submarine lay in peace negotiations. The

21. Erich Ludendorff, *Ludendorff's Own Story, August 1914—November 1918* (New York, Harper, 1920; 2 vols.), I, 363–370; Carnegie Endowment for International Peace, Division of International Law. *Preliminary History of the Armistice. Official Documents published by the German National Chancellery by order of the Ministry of State,* No. 38, p. 53. (Edited by James Brown Scott. New York, Oxford University Press, 1925.) Hereafter cited as *P.H.*

22. Friedrich von Payer, *Von Bethmann Hollweg bis Ebert* (Frankfurt, Frankfurter societäts-druckerei, 1923), p. 219.

Kaiser himself drafted a memorandum designed for Wilson's attention, giving warning that without an early peace the ruthless
warfare would be resumed. Wilson had been
meditating a public peace offer, but he felt
impelled to wait until after the national election. In the meantime the army and navy
chiefs, who were skeptical of the possibility
and perhaps the desirability of peace negotiations, pressed preparations for the submarine campaign. In November the Foreign
Secretary, Von Jagow, was forced out. He
was, according to Bernstorff, "the chief op-
ponent in Berlin of the submarine campaign,
and the pillar on which the idea of American
mediation rested. As long as Herr von Jagow
remained Secretary of State, a breach with
the United States was regarded as impossible."[23] The Chancellor still hoped for peace
negotiations. In order, as he expressed it, "to
have two irons in the fire," he decided to
state publicly Germany's willingness to
make peace, hoping that Wilson would support it. But he made the mistake of using a
tone that implied that the only peace Ger-

23. Bernstorff, *op. cit.*, p. 311.

many would consider would be that of a victor. In fact, as one studies the peace terms then drafted by the Germans it is clear that they would never have been accepted by the Allies until the latter were thoroughly defeated.

The effectiveness of Wilson's note of December 18 was largely nullified by the preceding German declaration. On the other hand, in Bernstorff's opinion, Wilson might have acted more promptly. Writing seventeen years later, he says:

The situation was as follows: Our navy demanded submarine warfare. Hindenburg and Ludendorff gave the decision for it, believing that they could this way bring about a victorious peace. The Emperor, Bethmann, Jagow and myself were against submarine warfare—because of U.S.A. . . . In those days Dr. Wilson was for the first time during the war really neutral, having discovered that both belligerents were equally bad or equally good (as you prefer expressing Wilson's opinion, and as the Treaty of Versailles and subsequent events have amply proved). Therefore, after his reëlection, Wilson should have come out immediately with his Peace Move. . . . In my opinion he waited too long, and during this time Jagow was turned out of office. Bethmann was too weak to oppose the Army and Navy. The Inevitable therefore had to happen.[24]

The army and navy chiefs did not give Bethmann a chance to develop the possibility of peace negotiations. Technical considerations made it important to begin the submarine campaign by February 1. Wilson had asked both sides to state their terms, in the hope of finding a middle ground. But Berlin hesitated. Despite the plea of Bernstorff that Germany state her terms privately and his insistence that if given time Wilson would find a way to open negotiations between the belligerents, he began to receive warnings from the German Foreign Office that the decision to renew the submarine campaign was under active consideration. That decision was taken definitely at a council at Pless on January 9, 1917. It was not until the nineteenth that Bernstorff received word that the unrestricted campaign would begin on February 1.

The Germans realized that the decision meant the entrance of the United States into

24. Bernstorff to C.S., June 12, 1933, *Amer. Dipl.,* pp. 185–186.

the war. Bernstorff cabled at once: "War inevitable in view of the proposed action."[25]
All the testimony of Bethmann before the
Reichstag investigating committee is col-
ored by his insistence that both the military
and political branches of the German Government were certain that the U-boat campaign meant war with the United States.[26]
In fact there was relief in some German
quarters at the thought that Wilson's efforts
to arrange peace would now be stopped. The
new Foreign Secretary of State, Zimmermann, told the budget committee of the
Reichstag that "the good thing" about the
rupture with America was that Germany
was finally rid of Wilson's efforts to mediate.[27] The inevitability of the break was a
matter of general assumption in Germany.
Bethmann later stated: "I am of the belief
that no doubt existed either in the minds of
the public on the whole, or in the minds of
the political parties, that the U-boat war
would ultimately bring the United States
into the war."[28]

25. Bernstorff, *op. cit.*, p. 359.
26. *G.D.*, I, 344.   27. *G.D.*, I, 409.
28. *G.D.*, I, 461.

Thus, when President Wilson, on receipt of the German declaration of unrestricted submarine warfare, ordered that Ambassador von Bernstorff be given his passports, it came as no surprise to the Germans. In view of the stand that the President had taken in the *Sussex* crisis, he could not do otherwise. In the circumstances, the rupture of diplomatic relations meant war. Ambassador Bernstorff says, after describing his handing in of the German statement:

Thus war was decided upon, even if it was not immediately declared. Everything that followed amounted only to preparation for war or war propaganda. Nothing except the abandonment of the U-boat campaign could have prevented war. It has frequently been asserted that the notorious Mexico telegram led to the war with the United States. I do not believe this is correct. The telegram was used with great success as propaganda against us; but the rupture of diplomatic relations—as I have already pointed out—was, in view of the situation, equivalent in all circumstances to war.[29]

To Wilson, the German declaration of unrestricted submarine warfare came as a ter-

29. Bernstorff, *op. cit.*, p. 380.

rible shock. All his papers show that at the moment his mind was concentrated upon peace mediation, and that he was determined to prevent American participation. Bernstorff testifies that at this time Wilson placed both groups of belligerents on the same plane. Only four weeks previous he had insisted to House that the nation would not enter the war—this was his own conviction and that of the people.[30] For three weeks he worked steadily to develop his peace proposals and on January 22 made his famous suggestion of compromise between the belligerents' terms: a "peace without victory." But the Germans, like the Allies, were unwilling to accept a peace without victory, for they believed that through the submarine, and despite the entrance of the United States, they could force a victorious peace.

Frequently the question is asked, What would have happened if the Germans had postponed or avoided the resumption of the unrestricted submarine campaign? Not infrequently of late, bold spirits have felt justified in replying that the United States would have entered the war, whatever Ger-

30. House Diary, January 4, 1917, *I.P.*, II, 412.

many's action, since they could not permit the defeat of the Allies.

No faithful historian can allow himself complete speculative luxury, for his business is with what happened and not what might have happened. Whatever comments he makes on the question must be couched in studiously undogmatic terms. Certain comments, however, are legitimate.

It is a fact that at the moment America entered the war the Allies were close to the end of their financial resources. We have it on the authority of Mr. Balfour, in June, that without immediate American assistance they faced "financial disaster which would be worse than defeat in the field."[31] They needed American credits above everything, and without them must ultimately have recognized the impossibility of victory. Lacking the essential American aid in finance, in food, in ships, would the British have agreed to negotiate a peace with Germany, in which France, Italy, and Russia would necessarily have concurred? Would Germany, grasping the possibility of a more complete victory than seemed within the realms of possibility

31. Balfour to House, June 29, 1917, *I.P.*, III, 101.

in December, have so stiffened her terms as to make a peace of negotiation impossible? Obviously, no answer can be given with confidence. The most reasonable is perhaps the one given in the German Admiralty Staff Memorials: a compromise in the early summer, but one tinged with a definite German advantage.

What would have been Wilson's attitude if the Germans had coöperated with his desire to end the war by mediation, if they had not launched the submarine campaign, and if the financial plight of the Allies had become apparent? In answering this question we are dealing with at least one solid fact in the midst of hypotheses: the character of Wilson. It is likely that he would have taken advantage of the increasing Allied weakness and pressed his peace proposals. The Allies would have had difficulty in repelling them. Grey has commented in his memoirs upon German obtuseness in interfering with Wilson's mediation by resuming the submarine campaign:

It is clear that Germany missed a great opportunity of peace. If she had accepted the Wilson policy, and was ready to agree to a Conference, the Allies could not have refused. They were dependent on American supplies; they could not have risked the ill-will of the Government of the United States, still less a *rapprochement* between the United States and Germany. Germans have only to reflect upon the peace that they might have had in 1916 compared with the peace of 1919.[32]

If, however, the Allies had refused peace mediation and the Germans had refrained from submarine warfare, would the United States have intervened to save the Allies? When the plight of the Allies became apparent there would certainly have come a demand from those who, like Page and Lansing, believed that our future was bound up with an Allied victory. Stress would certainly have been laid upon the community of economic interests between America and the Allies. There would have been open or concealed pressure for intervention. But it is difficult to see how such pressure could have become politically effective. The United States could not enter the war except on vote of Congress. Analysis of Congressional opinion reveals an overwhelming majority favor-

32. Edward Grey, 1st Viscount of Fallodon, *Twenty-Five Years 1892-1916* (New York, Stokes, 1925; 2 vols.), II, 135.

ing peace except upon the submarine issue. Congressmen would by no means have accepted either the political arguments of Page or the importance of Allied success to financial interests. Wilson himself could not have forced a vote for war.

But whatever can be said as to the pacific instincts of Congress can be repeated with heightened emphasis of Wilson. He had repeatedly displayed his disagreement with the attitude of Page and Lansing. He was entirely hostile to the idea that intervention should be based upon the material interests of the nation. To imagine that his pacifism could be touched by financial considerations is grotesque. Again and again he made clear that the United States ought not to be involved except upon the single issue of submarine sinkings. The fact was clear to the Germans. If they started the submarine campaign, it meant war with America. If they held back the campaign, there was no danger of American intervention.

III

GERMANY'S FATEFUL DECISION

WHATEVER disagreement there may be as to
the causes of American intervention in 1917,
there is unanimity as to the occasion. It was
the declaration of the unrestricted submarine campaign launched on February 1. The
assertion is frequently made that the submarine warfare was in turn caused by the
American export of munitions to the Allies.
This export, according to Senator Clark,
"ultimately led us into the war. . . . There
is no evidence whatever," he added, "to
show we would ever have entered in the war
or ever fired a gun except for that course of
action."[1] The declaration is obviously based
upon the assumption that had the United
States placed an embargo upon the sale of
munitions there would have been no unrestricted submarine warfare and thus no occasion for American intervention.

This point of view is worthy of study. It
raises the question as to the main purpose of

1. Statement before Senate munitions investigating committee, December 11, 1934.

the submarine. Was it designed primarily with a view to the interruption of the flow of munitions from the United States to Great Britain and France, or was it instituted with a broader aim? How far did the attitude and policy of the United States enter into the German calculations when they made the fateful decision? What could have been done by the United States that might have prevented Germany from resuming the unrestricted campaign on February 1, 1917?

Nearly all the answers attempted to such questions in this country have been based upon American sources or upon assumptions rather than facts as to the motivation of the submarine campaign. It is clearly desirable that we approach the problem from the German side. Fortunately, we have at our disposal a number of official German documents that bear directly upon the problem. Of particular value are the memoranda drafted by the German Admiralty Staff.

The unrestricted submarine campaign was started in February, 1915, by the German declaration of a war zone around the British Isles in which, beginning February 18, enemy commerce would be destroyed. It is true that the Germans hoped thereby to interrupt the import of American munitions by the Allies, who needed them badly. The chief immediate purpose of the campaign, however, was to bring pressure upon the Allies in order to compel them to relax their blockade. The German newspapers stressed the desirability of stopping the export of American munitions as well as the inhumanity of the Allied food blockade, as justification for the submarine; but the purpose of the articles was chiefly propagandist. According to the official German navy historian:

The first impulse to the German submarine warfare was given by the English declaration of November 2, 1914, proclaiming the North Sea to be a war zone, which contrary to international law affected not merely food going to Germany but all German imports. . . . It is true that the German official and unofficial reports emphasized the danger of starvation, but this was rather done with a propagandist eye to world opinion.[2]

From the log of the submarine commander who sank the *Lusitania*, it is obvious that

2. Statement of Admiral von Spindler, Yale House Collection; see also Tirpitz, *op. cit.*, II, 390–399.

the intensive campaign in the spring of 1915 was directed not merely, or even primarily, against ships carrying "munitions" in the narrow sense, but against all kinds of imports necessary to the life of Great Britain and coming from all over the world. It was designed to strike at the general economic capacity of the British to continue the war. This would be accomplished by wholesale destruction of cargo space upon which Great Britain depended for her necessities.[3]

The purpose of the submarine campaign is still more clearly evidenced by the official letters and "memorials" drafted by the German Admiralty Staff. The memorials of August 21, 1915, and of February 12, 1916, are devoted to analyses of the significant results of the submarine campaign. They deal not with the interruption of the import of ammunition—explosives and death-dealing instruments—but with the larger effects of the sinkings by submarines upon the economic life of the British, with especial emphasis upon the rise in prices and the shortage in foodstuffs. Admiral Holtzendorff's letter of December 22, 1916, referring to the "very

3. Log of Commander Schweiger, Yale House Collection.

purpose of the U-boat war," defines it as the bringing about of a "shortage in the necessary food products and raw-stuffs."[4]

Although the submarine campaign of 1915 failed to interrupt the flow of American munitions to the Allies, the German Admiralty Staff emphasized its relative success as a method of maritime warfare. "The U-boat War changed the economic situation of England from the ground up." Freight rates began to rise; there were advances in prices and shortage in meats. Even with the handicaps placed upon the free use of the submarine, resulting from American protests, the Admiralty Staff felt that the results obtained were of importance. "By means of a shortage which manifested itself principally in a notable increase of prices of essential foodstuffs and manufactured articles, and raw materials as well, it so damaged the commerce and trade of England that heavy economic and financial losses were felt in every direction."[5] The German Navy's criterion of success was thus much broader

4. Holtzendorff to Hindenburg, December 22, 1916, *G.D.*, II, 1221.
5. *G.D.*, II, 1222.

than merely the interruption of munitions traffic. Its ideal was the dislocation of British economic life in general, and it was just as important to disturb the industrial processes of that life in the British Isles as to win a military victory in France. "The commercial life of a country is like a masterpiece of higher mechanics," wrote the Chief of the Admiralty Staff in 1916, "let it once be disturbed, and there result a displacement of gears, friction, and breakage that continue without cessation. This was the result of the U-boat war last year which cannot be overestimated."[6]

The fact that the submarines did not accomplish even more than they did in 1915 was ascribed by the German naval tacticians to the political hindrances to their free use: the requirement of warning before attack, the necessity of sparing neutral shipping and, after the sinking of the *Lusitania* of sparing passenger liners.[7] The protests

6. *G.D.*, II, 1223.

7. The order to spare passenger ships was issued by the Kaiser June 5, 1915, but it was not published until after the sinking of the *Arabic* and the realization by Bernstorff that the United States was on the point of breaking diplomatic relations. Bernstorff, *op. cit.*, pp. 174–177.

raised by the navy leaders indicate the essential purpose of the submarine warfare. They objected to the sparing of passenger ships, not because they carried munitions, but because they resembled troop ships or freight vessels carrying food. Holtzendorff wrote:

The U-boat commanders were ordered to regard as passenger ships and to spare vessels which had certain characteristics; but at the same time these characteristics were shared by many and, indeed, important classes of freight steamers, as for instance cold-storage steamers for meat transportation. . . . There was also the impossibility of laying hold of steamers which were transporting troops and which appeared to be innocent passenger ships.

Another German disappointment lay in the failure to attain through the submarine campaign what the Admiralty Staff regarded as a "very material effect of the U-boat war, the psychological effect of worry," which they had hoped to impose upon the British, but which was alleviated by Wilson's protests against the submarine. The failure to interrupt the trade in ammunition was scarcely mentioned in the Admiralty Staff memorials.[8]

In February, 1916, following a comparative lull in submarine activity, Germany undertook the development of a much more vigorous campaign, based politically upon the contention that warning need not be given before an attack upon an armed merchantman, inasmuch as the armament carried was in fact not defensive but offensive and thereby changed the character of the merchantman into that of a war vessel. The strength of the submarines had been increased and their attacks became more deadly. In the spring of 1916, according to Admiral Michelsen "the submarines were just beginning to operate effectively again."[9] A memorial presented to the Government by the German Admiralty on February 12, 1916, advocated the resumption of a completely unrestricted campaign. The arguments therein advanced throw the clearest light on what the Admiralty Staff believed to be the crux of the whole question of bellig-

8. *G.D.*, II, 1222.
9. Michelsen, *op. cit.*, pp. 58–59.

erent trade and the vital purpose of the submarine campaign.

Those arguments are not concerned with
the desirability of cutting off ammunition in
the narrow sense, but with the possibility of
capitalizing the increasing lack of British
cargo space so as to throttle British economic life as a whole. They call attention to
the enormous increase in freight rates, from
three shillings per month for a twelve-month
Atlantic voyage, as the cost of carrying a ton
previous to the war, up to thirty shillings.
This tenfold increase, according to Admiral
Holtzendorff, was "the result and significant
expression of the shortage in cargo space.
Prices of merchandise rose accordingly. . . .
In addition thereto, there came about a dis-
quieting shortage in the stock of grain on
hand." Emphasizing the fact that by February, the shortage touched 56 per cent of
normal cargo space, the memorial insisted:

It follows that a new U-boat war would start
under conditions incomparably more favorable
than those existing in February, 1915, in view
of the fact that the cargo space still available for
the purpose of English imports and exports will
be unable to endure further appreciable losses

without affecting facilities for transporting absolutely essential imports and exports, and because England has been deprived of the greater part of its power of resistance by stringency, increase of prices and financial over-exertion. . . . If the new U-boat war is carried on ruthlessly, that is, on the basis that every craft in the war area will be subject to destruction, then the prospect is certain that, as the result of a shortage in freight space beyond her power of support, and a similar shortage in imports and exports and the resulting increases in price, and above all this, of being menaced by most dire financial perils, England will be forced to sue for peace within a definite period, and within six months at the longest.[10]

The German political leaders did not accede to this demand of the Admiralty for the resumption of an unrestricted submarine campaign. In fact in May, following the sinking of the *Sussex* and Wilson's threat of breaking diplomatic relations unless the Germans held by the rules of cruiser warfare, the Chancellor promised to give up the "sharpened" warfare against armed merchant ships and agreed that merchant vessels should not be sunk, without warning

10. *G.D.*, II, 1224.

and assurance of safety for the lives of passengers and crew.[11] This promise represented a temporary victory of Bethmann-
Hollweg and the Foreign Secretary, Von
Jagow, who maintained that the advantages of an unrestricted campaign could not
possibly outweigh the disadvantages of
American entrance into the war against
Germany. They realized from the dispatches
of Bernstorff that a resumption of the unrestricted campaign meant war with America.[12]

But as the summer of 1916 progressed the
political leaders found themselves under increasing pressure from public opinion and
from the technical naval leaders, who urged
that no attention be paid to Wilson, and that
Germany utilize every weapon that might
end the war shortly and successfully for
Germany. On the Western Front the German attack on Verdun had failed; the Allies
were pressing hard on the Somme; in August, Rumania entered the war against Germany; the pinch of the Allied blockade was
keenly felt. On the other hand, the cargo

11. *F.R.*, 1916, Supp., pp. 257–260.
12. Bernstorff, *op. cit.*, p. 250.

problem exercised continuous and increasingly intense effects upon the British. On August 27 the Admiralty Staff prepared for the Chancellor another memorial, reiterating the arguments of that of February 16 and emphasizing the fact that since February "enhancement of prices and shortage in England" threatened an economic crisis there.[13]

Two days later, August 29, 1916, the Supreme military command in Germany was given over to Hindenburg and Ludendorff. They were convinced that the unrestricted submarine campaign was essential to save Germany from defeat, but they did not believe that in view of the military situation of the moment, characterized by Allied pressure on the Somme and the threat of the Rumanian offensive, they could run the risk of bringing other European neutrals into the war. Hindenburg is recorded as saying to Ludendorff:

We would shout with joy if we could begin the U-boat war immediately, but it is a very serious question. We should have to take into consideration the possibility of new declarations of

13. *G.D.*, II, 1225.

war and of landings in Holland and Denmark. A
number of divisions would become tied up there
which we are not now in a position to spare. Our
allies are not to be trusted. The future is now
darker than ever. We shall have to let some time
pass.[14]

But during the autumn the situation improved for Germany. The Rumanian offensive was parried with unexpected success
and culminated in complete victory for the
Central Powers. The costly Allied drive on
the Somme failed to accomplish a rupture of
the German line. As a result of short crops
and continued losses of ships the British
food and cargo problem was still further intensified. In November, 1916, the German
military leaders agreed with the naval leaders that the unrestricted campaign should
be resumed in the spring, unless Bethmann's
attempts to bring about a peace conference
should prove successful. Hindenburg and
Ludendorff in their support of unrestricted
submarine warfare, naturally emphasized
the use of American shells by the Allies and
justified German resentment. Their testimony is more emotional in tone than the Ad-

14. *G.D.*, II, 857.

miralty Staff memorials. But Allied import
of munitions formed only a part of the reason for launching the submarine campaign.
Hindenburg said to the Reichstag committee:

It was our duty to conduct such a U-boat war,
since there were no other means at our disposal
for coming to the help of the hard-pressed western front, and for making our enemies, by belligerent methods, willing to consider peace. Moreover, this was the only way which could have
resulted in the termination of the war if the
peace proposal failed. Were we to put up quietly
with the fact that our sons and brothers on the
western front were to be torn to pieces by
American shells; were we to look upon the fact
with equanimity that, at home, our wives and
children were brought face to face with starvation as the result of the blockade of our cruel
opponents? If not, the U-boat war was the only
instrumentality by which we could oppose these
measures.[15]

Even more rhetorically General Ludendorff
exclaimed:

I remind you of the shells which were manufactured in the United States, and which bore the
American mark of manufacture; and I remem-

15. *G.D.*, II, 856.

ber the righteous anger which at that time was bound to flame in every soldier's heart.[16]

Apart from these two references the two military leaders indicated in their evidence that they approved the unrestricted campaign because they were anxious to adopt any measure that would give relief to the armies, and because this particular measure had the guaranty of the naval leaders. Ludendorff testified:

According to the judgment of the Navy, we were in possession of an instrumentality in the shape of the intensified U-boat war, which could bring us relief and which could preserve German lives and carry us to ultimate victory. In view of the situation in which we found ourselves, it was a duty which we owed the German nation and the Army to make use of the unrestricted U-boat war if the peace proposal was not accepted.[17]

But if the army leaders were thus emotionally vague, the Admiralty Staff was precise. On December 22, 1916, when it became evident that peace proposals would fail, Admiral Holtzendorff sent to Hindenburg a letter urging the immediate resump-

tion of the unrestricted submarine campaign
and a long memorial analyzing the situation
that, in his opinion, gave to the submarine
the opportunity to break the British defense.
Copies of these documents were sent to the
new Secretary of Foreign Affairs, Zimmermann, on January 6, 1917. They are of the
greatest historical value, since the fatal decision taken at Pless, on January 9, 1917,
approving the German Admiralty's policy,
was based upon the arguments contained
therein. From them we learn the essential
motives of the unrestricted submarine warfare.

Holtzendorff's letter begins with the statement that a definite decision of the war
must be reached before August 1, 1917, unless it is to result in the exhaustion of all
belligerents and "hence in a termination
which will be fatal for us."

Our enemies Italy and France have received
such a staggering blow, economically speaking,
that it is only by the energy and force of England that they are still kept on their feet. If we
can succeed in breaking the backbone of England's resistance, the war will immediately be
terminated in our favor. But the backbone of

England consists in the cargo space used for bringing to England those imports necessary for the maintenance of life, which assure her credit in foreign countries.[18]

The above paragraph is the text of all that follows. Emphasizing the diminution of available cargo space that had taken place in the preceding year and the general shortage of cargo space at the moment, Holtzendorff proceeds:

The abnormally poor results all over the world of this year's harvest of breadstuffs and provender has placed in our hands a very unique opportunity, of which no one will dare assume the responsibility of failing to take advantage. [As early as February, 1917] North America and Canada will be in a position of having practically no wheatstuffs at all to spare for the purposes of England. In this case, England must depend for its food supply on Argentina, separated as it is from England by a long trip, and since Argentina, as the result of its poor harvest, will be able to deliver but little, India and particularly Australia must be England's sources of supply.

Holtzendorff's letter repeats the phrase of the memorial of August 27, 1916: "Our ob-

18. *G.D.*, II, 1215–1219.

vious military task consists in the act of now bringing about a decision in our favor by the destruction of cargo space." Without cargo space England would not only be deprived of essential breadstuffs, but would also face a famine in fats, "since a third of the entire importations of butter into England come from Denmark and all the imported butter-fats come from Holland."

Further, it would mean an increased shortage of metals and woods as the result of the menace against the importations of metal and wood from Scandinavia going hand and hand with increased menace to shipment of metal from Spain. As a result, coal mining would decrease instantly, as the wood necessary for that purpose would no longer be available, and such would also be the case with iron and steel products and munitions dependant upon both of them. Finally, it would give us the opportunity so long desired to take effective steps against the importation of ammunition by neutrals, and to that extent to ease the burdens of the army. . . . Add to this the cessation of the psychological effects of panic and fear. These effects, which can be brought about only as the result of ruthless U-boat warfare, constitute in my opinion an absolutely essential prerequisite of success.

The interesting historical aspect of this

letter is that the desirability of the interruption of the import of ammunition is put in an entirely secondary position. The immediate and important effect of the unrestricted submarine campaign, in the mind of Holtzendorff, was to throw over England the fear of starvation. "I do not hesitate to declare," he wrote, "that as things stand at present, England will be forced to sue for peace within five months as the result of launching an unrestricted U-boat war." There is no reference to forcing peace on the military field by stopping the import of ammunition. All that such a stoppage would do would be "to ease the burdens of the army."

The dominating importance of the economic and particularly the food factors as the real motive of the unrestricted submarine campaign appears still more strikingly in the detailed memorial accompanying the above letter. This exhaustive document of more than thirty thousand words, after a survey of the cargo problem faced by the British up to the close of 1916, discusses the advisability of resuming the unrestricted submarine warfare under three heads: the food situation in England; tonnage; the question of politics. By far the most space is given to the first two sections. Under the first, the grain supply of England is analyzed, the threatening shortage exposed, possible substitutes considered, and the anxiety and depression resulting from famine emphasized. Brief reference is made to shortage in coal, wood, iron, cotton, wool, petroleum. The second section analyzes the cargo space available at the moment, with emphasis on "cargo-space famine," congestion at the ports, and the inevitably disastrous effects of an unrestricted submarine campaign upon cargo space. It reaches the conclusion that because of rapidly increasing shortage England would suffer from lack of grains, other foodstuffs, metals, cotton; from the collapse of the English cattle-raising industry and the breakdown of shipbuilding; and that "English finance will stand or fall on the question of the English export trade." Only at the end of the section is there in a single sentence any reference to the advantageous effect of striking at "the American importations of war material and war stuffs for the purposes of the British munitions industry." It is placed in an inconspicuous paragraph and subordinated to the advantages that would result from the possibility of freely sinking military transports in the Channel and the Mediterranean.

The third section of the memorial is devoted chiefly to an estimate of the disadvantages that would result from the entrance of the United States into the war on the side of the Allies. There is again one brief reference to making "available for the Navy the very welcome opportunity of sinking shipments of ammunition." The conclusion is that the evil of bringing the United States into the war is less than the danger faced by Germany if the war of exhaustion is to continue. There are appended to the memorial detailed notes on the British wheat supply, the shortage of American and Canadian grain, the capacity of Argentina, India, and Australia to supply English grain necessities.[19]

Careful study of the Admiralty Staff documents compels the conclusion that the main motive behind the resumption of the unrestricted submarine war in 1917 was the

19. Text of the Admiralty Staff Memorial, *G.D.*, II, 1226–1277.

conviction that England could be starved, or at least threatened so clearly with starvation as to be willing to consider peace. This conclusion is confirmed by the testimony given by Admiral Koch before the investigating committee. He defines the purpose of the submarine campaign as

the plan of undertaking every month to deliver a vigorous cut at the arteries of England's economic existence in order to disgust England with its operations at long range against Germany and with the war that lasted year after year, and to show England that, just as the throttling process worked against us, the constant gnawing at the source of England's economic life worked against her.[20]

Dr. Helfferich, who had been Minister of the Interior at the time of the declaration of unrestricted submarine warfare, was later called upon by the investigating committee to explain why he had yielded his opposition to the declaration and supported the policy of the navy leaders. He based his explanation upon the food situation in England and the increased efficiency of the submarines, which, in combination, opened the possibil-

20. *G.D.*, I, 618.

ity of ruining the economic life of the British
Isles by an elimination of the necessary
cargo space. Food and not ammunition was
the vital problem.

> The commercial conditions . . . had undergone
> a change in favor of the adoption of the unre-
> stricted U-boat war, mainly as the result of the
> poor harvests all over the world, and particu-
> larly as the result of the bad harvests in Eng-
> land and of the ruinously bad harvests in the
> United States and Canada.[21]

The historian must thus conclude that the
unrestricted submarine campaign resulted
from much wider and more complicated conditions than the American export of ammunition. The German documents by no means
bear out Senator Clark's impression that
there is "no evidence whatever" to show we
would have entered the war except for that
export. The submarine campaign, according
to those who planned it, was designed to
sever all the arteries of British economic life.
"Are we . . . in a position," wrote Von
Haniel, Counsellor of the German Embassy
at Washington, "to cut England off so completely from all imports that she will be

21. *G.D.,* II, 818.

obliged to conclude peace within a short time?"[22] "The only justification for the resumption of unrestricted U-boat warfare," wrote Under-Secretary of State Albert, "would be the possibility of an actual isolation of England for a period of from at least four to six months."[23]

An American embargo upon munitions in the narrow sense would have had very slight deterrent effect upon the German naval leaders. Even an absolute embargo upon all American exports to the Allies, including foodstuffs, would not have touched the main points raised in the Admiralty Staff decisions. American harvests were so bad that such an embargo at that moment would have seemed of comparatively slight importance. The Staff memorials laid far more stress upon the Argentine and India as sources of supply. A general embargo upon exports would have given the German leaders pause only as an indication that Wilson was prepared to bring pressure upon the Allies for peace.

In December, 1916, Germany saw the need of immediate peace. If she could secure

22. *G.D.*, II, 869.   23. *G.D.*, II, 872.

it through the mediation of Wilson she would hold back her submarines. Otherwise, she would break the backbone of the British by the submarine attack on cargo space, and would not be stopped by American concessions or American threats.

IV

MISINTERPRETED DOCUMENTS

THE citation of documentary evidence is an essential part of the writing of history. It goes without saying that it is worse than valueless if it is associated with unskilful or hasty interpretation of the documents. Accurate history demands an understanding of the background and a capacity for objective analysis of the document utilized. In the discussions of the problems of American neutrality from 1914 to 1917, three documents have received especial attention as throwing light upon the factors that forced the United States into war. They are the Page cablegram of March 5, 1917; the Wilson St. Louis speech of September 5, 1919; and the Lansing letter of September 6, 1915. Very broad generalizations have been based upon them. It is the purpose of the following pages to test the validity of such generalizations and to assess the historical significance of the documents.

I.

THE PAGE CABLEGRAM OF MARCH 5, 1917

This document has been widely quoted recently as evidence of the compelling influence of economic interests in bringing the United States into the war. It is a telegram from Walter Hines Page, American Ambassador in Great Britain, to the Secretary of State, suggesting the probability of a collapse of Allied credit and emphasizing the danger to American economic interests, which depended upon trade with the Allies. It closes with the further suggestion that by entering the war America might avert an economic disaster. It was sent a month after the dismissal of Bernstorff. The salient passages from the telegram follow:

The financial inquiries made here reveal an international condition most alarming to the American financial and industrial outlook. England is obliged to finance her allies as well as to meet her own war expenses. She has as yet been able to do these tasks out of her own resources. But in addition to these tasks she cannot continue her present large purchases in the United States without shipments of gold to pay for them and she cannot maintain large shipments of gold for two reasons: first, both England and France must retain most of the gold they have to keep their paper money at par; and second, the submarine has made the shipping of gold too hazardous, even if they had it to ship. The almost immediate danger, therefore, is that Franco-American and Anglo-American exchange will be so disturbed that orders by all the Allied Governments will be reduced to the lowest minimum and there will be almost a cessation of transatlantic trade. This will, of course, cause a panic in the United States. . . . This condition may soon come suddenly unless action is quickly taken to prevent it. France and England must have a large enough credit in the United States to prevent the collapse of world trade and of the whole of European finance.

If we should go to war with Germany the greatest help we could give the Allies would be such a credit. In that case our Government could, if it would, make a large investment in a Franco-British loan or might guarantee such a loan. All the money would be kept in our own country, trade would be continued and enlarged till the war ends, and after the war, Europe would continue to buy food and would buy from us also an enormous supply of things to re-equip her peace industries. We should thus reap the profit of an uninterrupted, perhaps an enlarging, trade over a number of years and we should hold their securities in payment.

But if we hold most of the money and Europe cannot pay for re-equipment there may be a world-wide panic for an indefinite period.

Unless we go to war with Germany our Government of course cannot make such a direct grant of credit, but is there no way in which our Government might indirectly, immediately, help the establishment in the United States of a large Franco-British credit without a violation of armed neutrality? . . . I think that the pressure of this approaching crisis has gone beyond the ability of the Morgan Financial Agency for the British and French Governments. The need is becoming too great and urgent for any private agency to meet, for every such agency has to encounter jealousies of rivals and of sections.

Perhaps our going to war is the only way in which our present preeminent trade position can be maintained and a panic averted. The submarine has added the last item to the danger of a financial world crash. During a period of uncertainty about our being drawn into the war, no more considerable credit can be privately placed in the United States and a collapse may come in the meantime.[1]

From the above document the conclusion has been drawn that America entered the

1. Text in *F.R.*, 1917, Supp. 2, Vol. I, p. 516. Also in Burton J. Hendrick, *Life and Letters of Walter Hines Page* (New York, Doubleday, Page, 1922–25; 3 vols.), II, 269–271.

war in order to maintain Allied credit and American trade; that through the pressure of hidden financial interests President Wilson was compelled to yield his determination that the United States remain neutral. Extravagant statements have been made. "When Americans went into the fray," said Senator Nye, "they little thought that they were there and fighting to save the skins of American bankers who had bet too boldly on the outcome of the war and had two billions of dollars of loans to the Allies in jeopardy." And on another occasion: "It was sales and shipments and the financing of munitions and contraband and the lure for profit that drew us into the last war."[2] A yet more extreme conclusion is that of Mr. Barnes: "The American documents show that Page and Wilson discussed our entry in terms of British credit and the status of American international bankers."[3]

The Page cable is not a new discovery. It was printed by Mr. Burton Hendrick some thirteen years ago and has been at the dis-

2. Radio addresses, June 7, August 27, 1935.
3. Harry Elmer Barnes, *History of Western Civilization* (New York, Harcourt, 1935), p. 605.

posal of historians ever since. They have
been cautious in the conclusions drawn from
it. They have regarded it as useful commen-
tary upon the crisis that might be faced by
the Allies if the war continued and if they
could not finance a continuance of their purchasing program. But no serious historian
has suggested that the telegram implied that
American interests in Allied loans were en-
dangered, or that there was any concern
about the loans already outstanding, which
enjoyed a ready market. Any American in-
vestor could go into the market with his Allied bonds and get what he paid for them.

Mr. Page's cable is very poor evidence,
furthermore, of the assertion that American
policy was controlled by the "financing of
munitions and contraband." He was himself
by no means an expert in political economy,
had little or no connection with financial
interests, and, as all the documents indicate,
he was in no position to appreciate the factors affecting policy in Washington. He admitted his failure to understand Wilson. He
would be the last witness to be called to explain Wilson's policy. So much, historians
have taken for granted. It remained for

Senator Nye to aver, "Walter Hines Page, our Ambassador to Great Britain, best tells us what was moving us into the war."

Ambassador Page had for some time advocated American intervention on the side of the Allies in order to cement the bonds of Anglo-American friendship which he believed to be the chief guaranty of a peaceful and prosperous future. He was clearly not uninclined to utilize arguments based upon economic factors to reinforce his sentimental attitude. But of all Americans connected with the Government he was the least likely to exercise any influence upon Wilson. As far back as October, 1914, the President confessed that he was "disturbed" by Page's pro-British attitude. In the summer of 1916, the President brought Page home for a vacation in the hope, as he expressed it, "that he may get back a little way at least to the American point of view about things."[4] Page's advice to Wilson, tinged by pro-British sentiments, had upon him an effect the opposite of that intended. Mr. Lansing writes:

4. Wilson to House, October 18, 1915, July 23, 1916, Yale House Collection.

One of the chief results of Mr. Page's visit to the United States and of the conferences which he had with Mr. Wilson was, unless I am greatly mistaken, to make the President more than ever irritated against the British. . . . His insistence on our adopting the British way of looking at the situation stirred the ire of the President and made him stubborn.[5]

There is no evidence that Page's cable affected the policy of the United States in any respect. Doubtless it was read by the Secretary of State, and presumably its contents discussed with the Secretary of the Treasury. Much of the information it contains must have already been at their disposal. The threat to the transportation of gold presented by the submarine was obvious. All America could see, furthermore, that the submarine campaign was striking directly at American exports and throwing American business into confusion. American ports were in a state of virtual blockade, since shippers were afraid to send out cargoes without protection. The ports were jammed and freights becoming snarled.

5. Robert Lansing, *War Memoirs of Robert Lansing* (Indianapolis and New York, Bobbs-Merrill, 1935), pp. 170–171.

In any case, the cable seemed to the Secretary of State of such relative unimportance that he did not bother to answer it or suggest any plan for the facilitation of Allied credits. On March 9, four days after the original cable, the Ambassador followed it with a reference to a conference with the Governor of the Bank of England, in which the danger to Allied financing of purchases was further emphasized, and a request for instructions as to the possibility of the Reserve banks rediscounting ninety-day bills. To neither of these cables, it would seem, was any reply vouchsafed, since on March 24, nearly three weeks after the first cable, Mr. Page refers back to them and intimates that "some answer" would be "advantageous."[6]

The truth was, and it is attested frequently in Mr. Page's own correspondence, that neither the State Department nor the President paid much attention to the Ambassador's advice; his telegrams certainly cannot be cited as evidence of factors bringing the United States into the war. Wilson

6. *F.R.*, 1917, Supp. 2, Vol. I, pp. 518, 519; House Diary, March 19, 1917; Lansing, *op. cit.*, pp. 235-236.

was facing the supreme decision and all available sources show that he made it on his own responsibility. When it was made he confessed privately, and later in public, the factors that proved compelling. Never did he refer, so far as our evidence goes, to any of the commercial arguments advanced by Mr. Page. Never did he intimate that material interests had the slightest influence in the decision he reached. "Nothing except the abandonment of the U-boat campaign," said Bernstorff, "could have prevented war."[7] Wilson confessed the same thought to the editor of the *World* on the eve of his war speech.[8]

2.

WILSON'S ST. LOUIS SPEECH OF
SEPTEMBER 5, 1919

President Wilson dominated the foreign policy of the United States. He is universally recognized as the most important personal factor in the decision that brought America into the war, and his testimony as to the motives of intervention is clearly of the highest value. That testimony is given repeatedly in

7. *Op. cit.*, p. 380.   8. Heaton, *op. cit.*, pp. 268–270.

many of his private and public papers. Invariably, the President stressed motives other than material. Students of Wilson's political philosophy are agreed that his policy was based upon a principle which he enunciated at the beginning of his term of office, before the outbreak of the World War: "It is a very perilous thing," he said at Mobile, October 27, 1913, "to determine the foreign policy of a nation in the terms of material interest."[9]

It is surprising therefore, to find recent interpreters of the events that brought us into the war citing President Wilson as a witness to the contention that we were led to war by commercial motives. It is still more surprising to find such critics of Wilson's policy implying that the President and his advisers were guilty of deliberate fraud in concealing from the people the commercial purpose for which they were fighting. "It was only after the war," Senator Nye remarks, "that President Wilson confessed that he knew what it was all about." To support this accusation of fraud and to substantiate the thesis that America entered the war

9. Baker and Dodd, edd., *op. cit.*, I, 67.

from commercial motives and that Wilson
knew it, Senator Nye cites the following ex-
cerpt from Wilson's speech at St. Louis, September 5, 1919:

Why, my fellow citizens, is there any man here
or any woman,—let me say is there any child
here,—who does not know that the seed of war
in the modern world is industrial and commercial rivalry? The real reason that the war that
we have just finished took place was that Germany was afraid her commercial rivals were going to get the better of her, and the reason why
some nations went into the war against Germany
was that they thought Germany would get the
commercial advantage of them. The seed of jealousy, the seed of deep-seated hatred, was hot
successful commercial and industrial rivalry.
This war in its inception was a commercial and
industrial war. It was not a political war.[10]

Senator Nye's interpretation of the fore-
going passage is as follows:

Ah! The rulers of the world, the foreign offices,
the State Departments, the Presidents and
Kings and Czars and Kaisers knew what the
war was about all the time. . . . There was

10. Text of the speech in *Congressional Record* (Washington, Government Printing Office), LVIII, 5005–5008.
Senator Nye has inserted the words "in its inception," which
do not appear in the *Congressional Record*.

fraud perpetrated by the governments of the world in hiding from their people the economic causes for which they were fighting.[11]

The charge of fraudulent concealment thus leveled against President Wilson and the State Department is very ill-supported by the particular document chosen as evidence. Analysis of the speech as a whole shows that Wilson is making a sharp differentiation between the motives underlying the action of European nations which embarked upon the European war in 1914 and the basic motives of American policy, which, he insists, are of a different kind. Just because they are different, he argues, we are trusted by the other nations who look to us to lead in the movement for world peace. He warns his hearers that if we permit the United States to follow a selfish course, if we say "we are in this world to live by ourselves and get what we can out of it by any selfish processes—then the reaction will change the whole heart and attitude of the world toward this great free, justice-loving people."

The paragraph cited by Senator Nye must be analyzed with the distinction made by

11. Address at Carnegie Hall, May 27, 1935.

Wilson between the traditional idealism of
America and the material causes of war in
Europe. In that paragraph he is obviously
referring to the causes of the European war
and not to our intervention in 1917. This is
perfectly clear from a passage in this paragraph which, as delivered, came between the
sentences cited by Senator Nye, but which
Senator Nye saw fit to omit from his quota-
tion. The deleted passage refers to German
jealousy of Belgian industry as a cause of
German aggression and makes perfectly
clear that the President had European and
not American conditions in mind; Senator
Nye's interpretation is possible only if it is
omitted. Furthermore, even in the quoted
sentences, Wilson refers to "some nations"
that went to war against Germany lest Germany gain commercial advantage. To in-
clude the United States in his thought with
those nations, would denature the sense of
the sentence. If he had wished to make a
"confession," there would have been the
place for a direct reference to America.

It is not necessary to twist the meaning of
Wilson's speeches to discover what he regarded as the motive for our intervention in

the World War. His opinion is expressed with crystal clarity, in a multitude of speeches after the war, both before and after this St. Louis speech. On July 10, 1919, when presenting the Treaty to the Senate, immediately after his return from Europe, he said:

The United States entered the war upon a different footing from every other nation except our associates on this side of the sea. We entered it, not because our material interests were directly threatened or because any special treaty obligations to which we were parties had been violated, but only because we saw the supremacy, and even the validity, of right everywhere put in jeopardy and free government likely to be everywhere imperiled by the intolerable aggression of a power which respected neither right nor obligation. . . . We entered the war as the disinterested champions of right and we are interested ourselves in the terms of peace in no other capacity.[12]

In an address given on the same day and in the same city as that quoted by Senator Nye, President Wilson declared that the American people had gone to war "to see to it that nobody after Germany's defeat

12. *Congressional Record,* LVIII, 2336–2339.

should repeat the experiment which Germany had tried."[13] At Columbus, on September 4, speaking of the right of peoples "to live their own lives under the governments which they themselves choose to set up," as vindicated by the results of the war, he said, "That is the American principle and I was glad to fight for it." And with reference to men who opposed the League of Nations, he concluded, "Do not let them lead this Nation away from the high purposes with which this war was inaugurated and fought."[14] In his Jackson Day letter of January 8, 1920, he stated, "This Nation entered the Great War to vindicate its own rights and to protect and preserve free government."[15] In his message of May 28, 1920, to Congress he said: "We entered the war most reluctantly. Our people were profoundly disinclined to take part in a European war, and at last did so only because they became convinced that it could not in truth be regarded as only a European war, but must be regarded as a war in which civilization itself was involved

13. Address at luncheon at Hotel Statler, St. Louis, *Congressional Record*, LVIII, 5003–5005.
14. *Congressional Record*, LVIII, 4997–5000.
15. *Idem*, LIX, p. 1249.

and human rights of every kind as against a belligerent government." In that same message he listed the specific purposes "we professed to be seeking" when we entered the war. None of them has any relationship with commercial factors.[16]

With such plenitude of positive evidence there can be little doubt of Wilson's understanding of the motives that led him, a sincere pacifist, to accept the inevitability of American intervention. It is not difficult to imagine the horror he would experience at the suggestion that he took us into the struggle, as Senator Nye insisted, "to save the skins of bankers."[17] The alleged confession of the St. Louis speech was actually nonexistent. The accusation of fraud against the President, of concealing from the people the cause for which they were fighting, is palpably without basis.

3.

THE LANSING LETTER OF SEPTEMBER 6, 1915

In the summer of 1935 there was presented to the Foreign Relations Committee

16. *Idem*, pp. 7747–7748.
17. Address at Carnegie Hall, May 27, 1935.

of the Senate an unpublished document of
the first importance. This was a letter from
Secretary of State Lansing to President
Wilson, dated September 6, 1915, regarding
the desirability of prohibiting private general loans to the belligerent governments.
Its publication lifts much of the mist which
has hung over the process which changed
United States policy in regard to loans from
the position adopted in the first weeks of the
war to that approved in the autumn of 1915.

On August 15, 1914, the State Department issued an answer to the inquiry made
by bankers as to the attitude of the Government in case they were asked to make loans
to foreign governments: "There is no reason
why loans should not be made to the governments of neutral nations, but in the judgment of this Government, loans by American
bankers to any foreign nation which is at
war are inconsistent with the true spirit of
neutrality."[18] The statement was signed by
Mr. Bryan, then Secretary of State, and obviously reflected his philosophy. He feared
lest the loaning of money to belligerents
would give the Americans a material interest

18. *F.R.*, 1914, Supp., p. 580.

in the cause of the nation to whom they lent; and that the country "would be divided up into groups, each group engaged in negotiating loans to the belligerent countries with which it sympathized."[19] In his *Memoirs* Mr. Bryan pictures the President as ardently in agreement with the policy of frowning upon general loans to the belligerents. The Administration was soon forced to modify its attitude. In October, 1914, Wilson authorized Lansing to intimate that "credit loans" were permissible, and bank credits were almost immediately extended to belligerent governments. The first loan of all to be put on public sale was a loan to Germany. On March 31, 1915, the State Department declared that it had neither approved or disapproved credit loans. Finally, on September 14, 1915, the State Department permitted the press to state that the general loan for which the Anglo-French commission was negotiating would not be opposed.[20]

The letter from Mr. Lansing to President

19. William Jennings Bryan and Mary Baird Bryan, *The Memoirs of William Jennings Bryan* (Philadelphia, Winston, 1925), p. 375.

20. *F.R.*, 1915, Supp., p. 820; *New York Times*, October 16, 1914, October 14, 1915.

Wilson, of September 6, 1915, explains the conditions which led the State Department to modify the attitude taken a year previous by Mr. Bryan. It is of sufficient importance to be read as a whole:[21]

Doubtless Secretary McAdoo has discussed with you the necessity of floating government loans for the belligerent nations, which are purchasing such great quantities of goods in this country, in order to avoid a serious financial situation which will not only affect them but this country as well.

Briefly the situation, as I understand it, is this: Since Dec. 1, 1914, to June 30, 1915, our exports have exceeded our imports by nearly a billion dollars, and it is estimated that the excess will be from July 1 to Dec. 31, 1915, a billion and three quarters. Thus for the year 1915 the excess will be approximately two and half billions of dollars.

It is estimated that the European banks have about three and a half billions of dollars in gold in their vaults. To withdraw any considerable amount would disastrously affect the credit of the European nations, and the consequence would be a general state of bankruptcy.

If the European countries cannot find means to pay for the excess of goods sold to them over those purchased from them, they will have to

21. Text of letter in *New York Times*, August 19, 1935.

stop buying and our present export trade will shrink proportionately. The result would be restriction of outputs, industrial depression, idle capital and idle labor, numerous failures, financial demoralization, and general unrest and suffering among the laboring classes.

Probably a billion and three-quarters of the excess of European purchases can be taken care of by the sale of American securities held in Europe and by the transfer of trade balances of Oriental countries, but that will leave three-quarters of a billion to be met in some other way. Furthermore, even if that is arranged, we will have to face a more serious situation in January, 1916, as the American securities held abroad will have been exhausted.

I believe that Secretary McAdoo is convinced and I agree with him that there is only one means of avoiding this situation which would so seriously affect economic conditions in this country, and that is the flotation of large bond issues by the belligerent governments. Our financial institutions have the money to loan and wish to do so.

On account of the great balance of trade in our favor, the proceeds of these loans would be expended here. The result would be a maintenance of the credit of the borrowing nations based on their gold reserve, a continuance of our commerce at its present volume and industrial activity, with the consequent employment of capital and labor and national prosperity.

In October, 1914, after a conference with you, I gave my "impressions" to certain New York bankers in reference to "credit loans," but the general statement remained unaffected. In drafting the letter of Jan. 20, 1915, to Senator Stone I sought to leave out a broad statement and to explain merely the reasons for distinguishing between "general loans" and "credit loans." However, Mr. Bryan thought it well to repeat the August declaration and it appears in the first sentence of Division 13 of the letters, a copy of which I enclose.

On March 31, 1915, another press statement was given out from the department which read as follows:

"The State Department has from time to time received information directly or indirectly to the effect that belligerent nations had arranged with banks in the United States for credits in various sums. While loans to belligerents have been disapproved, this government has not felt that it was justified in interposing objection to the credit arrangements which have been brought to its attention. It has neither approved these nor disapproved—it has simply taken no action in the premises and expressed no opinion."

Manifestly, the government has committed itself to the policy of discouraging general loans to belligerent governments. The practical reasons for the policy at the time we adopted it were sound, but basing it on the ground that loans are "inconsistent with the true spirit of neutrality" is now a source of embarrassment. This latter ground is as strong today as it was a year ago, while the practical reasons for discouraging loans have largely disappeared.

We have more money than we can use. Popular sympathy has become crystallized in favor of one or another of the belligerents to such an extent that the purchase of bonds would in no way increase the bitterness of partisanship or cause a possibly serious situation.

Now, on the other hand, we are face to face with what appears to be a critical economic situation, which can only be relieved, apparently, by the investment of American capital in foreign loans to be used in liquidating the enormous balance of trade in favor of the United States.

Can we afford to let a declaration as to our conception of the "true spirit of neutrality," made in the first days of the war, stand in the way of our national interests which seem to be seriously threatened?

If we cannot afford to do this, how are we to explain away the declaration and maintain a semblance of consistency?

My opinion is that we ought to allow the loans to be made for our own good. I have been seeking some means of harmonizing our policy, so

unconditionally announced, with the flotation of
general loans. As yet I have found no solution to
the problem.

Secretary McAdoo considers that the situation is becoming acute and that something
should be done at once to avoid the disastrous
results which will follow a continuance of the
present policy.

Two important conclusions have been
drawn from this document by those who
presented it to the Foreign Relations Committee of the Senate. The first is that the
economic interests of the country proved to
be of such power that we were drawn into
what amounted to an economic alliance with
Great Britain and France, although our true
political interests demanded that we remain
as isolated from them as from Germany. If
we had held to Mr. Bryan's original attitude,
they maintain, trade with the Allies would
have collapsed, a preferable misfortune, if
even that, to intervention in the war. Because of the economic alliance that developed, according to this thesis, we had to
fight.

There can be no question, certainly, of the
importance of the economic interests of the

country in the mind of Lansing; such factors must have weighed appreciably with the President, who approved the new policy. They were thinking, it is obvious, not of any special interests such as munitions makers or bankers, but of the economic welfare of the nation as a whole. The effect of a collapse of foreign trade, as Lansing insisted in his letter to Wilson, would be "restriction of outputs, industrial depression, idle capital and idle labor, numerous failures, financial demoralization and general unrest and suffering among the laboring classes." Even so, had Mr. Wilson believed there to have been an inevitable connection between our trade with the Allies and our ultimate intervention, it is likely that he would not have approved the new policy. But for him, as for most Americans, our right to maintain commercial relations with Great Britain and France was clear; it had been admitted by the Germans; they had made no intimation that they would regard it as cause for war. At this very moment, in September, 1915, Bernstorff was on the point of accepting the essence of Wilson's contentions regarding submarine warfare. As matters later devel-

oped the submarine warfare was motivated
not merely by American exports but by the
larger design of the complete isolation of the
British Isles from all the world.[22]

Even admitting that a continuance of the
prohibition of loans might have removed the
motivation of the submarine warfare, Mr.
Lansing's letter indicates clearly the practical impossibility of such a policy. The conclusion has been drawn from the letter that
it proves the necessity of an automatic imposition of embargoes upon exports and
loans. In a letter to the chairman of the Foreign Relations Committee, Senators Clark
and Nye assert: "With these official statements before us, it is an inescapable conclusion that the policy of the United States
must be fixed before the declaration of an
European war or not be fixed at all. In that
event, we face the danger of drifting into another European war as we did before."[23]

The declaration that we "drifted" into the
war is quite without evidence. Historians
are agreed that our relations with Germany
were more friendly and those with the Allies

22. *Supra,* pp. 76–80.
23. Letter of Senators Clark and Nye, *New York Times,*
August 19, 1935.

less friendly immediately preceding the rupture. That rupture came suddenly as the result of the resumption of the submarine campaign.

We may put on one side for the moment the assertion, entirely lacking in supporting evidence, that we "drifted" into the war. Does the Lansing letter admit the possibility of "fixing" a policy before the declaration of a European war with the implication that such a policy can remain fixed? The whole tenor of the document is to the effect that a policy which is designed to put into effect automatically certain measures such as embargoes upon loans cannot stand up against the force of circumstances. It is possible to set up a policy that is "fixed" but the difficulty is to keep it fixed when conditions make it appear undesirable. "Can we afford," wrote Mr. Lansing, "to let a declaration as to our conception of the 'true spirit of neutrality,' made in the first days of the war, stand in the way of our national interests which seem to me seriously threatened?" The same question and the inevitable negative answer can be applied to a policy arrived at before war breaks out.

If, therefore, the Lansing document is worth anything as a guide, it is that a pious declaration such as that of Mr. Bryan, if it come into conflict with an interest that had not crystallized when the declaration was made, will cause a situation which in the letter is described as "embarrassing." More than that: no embarrassment is going to prevent the abrogation of the declaration as soon as it becomes apparent that it does not accord with the national interest. The Bryan declaration was modified to accord with changing circumstances during the autumn of 1914 and the spring of 1915. It was wiped out in the autumn of 1915 because it did not run along with the welfare of the nation.

Hardly of less significance is Mr. Lansing's confession that the Bryan policy of discouraging general loans had not served to promote "the true spirit of neutrality." So far as the spirit of partisanship was concerned, he believed that it made little or no difference in September, 1915, whether or not general loans were approved: "Popular sympathy has become crystallized in favor of one or another of the belligerents to such an extent that the purchase of bonds would in no way increase the bitterness of partisanship or cause a possibly serious situation."

The opinion of the Secretary of State would thus coincide with the historical conclusions based upon study of numerous documents: that partisanship resulted primarily from emotional and political factors, and not from financial affiliations. At the time of the first Bryan declaration, long before any attempt had been made by German or Allied propaganda agencies, opinion had set in favor of one side or the other. The unpleasant reaction on the eastern seaboard to the German invasion of Belgium helped to form an opinion favoring the Allies that could not be touched either by Wilson's adjuration to be neutral in thought as well as in deed nor by the prohibition on loans. Before the government ban on general loans had been raised, anti-German opinion was stimulated by the sinking of the *Lusitania*. The success of the first Anglo-French loan was doubtless stimulated by this feeling, but it had nothing to do with causing it. As Lansing observed, popular sympathy had already become crystallized.

V

INFLUENCES OF TRADE WITH THE ALLIES ON AMERICAN DIPLOMACY, 1914–17

THE importance of economic factors in the trend of diplomatic relations needs no emphasis. It was tremendously intensified during the years of American neutrality when, under conditions of the utmost difficulty, the United States attempted to maintain its trade with Germany either directly or through the neutrals, and developed rapidly its commerce with the Allies. Our interest, both material and legal, in preserving lawful commercial relations with Germany, led to a spirited diplomatic contest with the Allies. It threatened, especially in the early autumn of 1916, to result in the imposition of embargoes on exports; it might have created a diplomatic crisis. On the other hand, our economic welfare demanded cordial relations with the Allies and the avoidance of a diplomatic conflict that might interfere with our trade. In the end, America not merely kept on friendly terms with the Allies but by entering the war threw in its political fortunes with them.

The question arises as to whether the issue was decided on purely economic grounds, or whether other factors played a rôle of importance. To answer this question it is necessary first to survey the influences which constantly tended to disturb diplomatic relations between the United States and the Allies; and then to consider the counteracting factors that prevented us from pushing our dispute with them to the point of imposing embargoes or prohibiting loans.

At the very beginning of the war, American official relations with the Allies were dominated by commercial issues. The refusal of the British and French to approve the Declaration of London without denaturing reservations, the extension of the contraband list, the development of the right of visit and search, harassed American trade. On December 26, 1914, the State Department dispatched a general note of protest against Allied methods of interference with neutral commerce.[1] Wilson regarded this dispute over trade rights very seriously. On

1. *F.R.*, 1914, Supp., pp. 372–375.

September 30 he commented on the difficulties that led to the War of 1812 with England and Madison's desire to avoid war: "Madison and I are the only two Princeton men that have become President. The circumstances of the War of 1812 and now run parallel. I sincerely hope they will not go further."[2] We have already noted that Wilson was bothered because Ambassador Page did not take the defense of American economic rights more seriously.

I am a little disturbed by the messages Walter Page is sending recently. It is very necessary that he should see the difficult matters between us and the British Government in the light in which they are seen on this side of the water, and I am sorry that he should think the argument of them from our point of view the work of mere "library lawyers." . . . It would be very unfortunate if he were to become unsympathetic or were to forget the temper of folks at home, who are exceedingly sensitive about every kind of right.[3]

On November 3 the British Ambassador, Sir Cecil Spring Rice, bore testimony to the

2. *I.P.*, I, 303–304.
3. Wilson to House, October 23, 1914, *Amer. Dipl.*, p. 57.

importance of economic factors on the diplomatic situation:

The American conscience is on our side, but the American pocket is being touched. Copper and oil are dear to the American heart and the export is a matter of great importance. We are stopping this export and the consequence is a steady howl which is increasing in volume. We should probably do the same. But the howl may become very furious soon.[4]

It is true that Ambassador Page at London wished to eliminate economic factors. "A cargo of copper, I grant you, may be important; but it can't be as important as our friendship." But this point of view was never accepted by the State Department or by Wilson. The latter, during the spring of 1915, endeavored by private negotiation to secure concessions from the Allies which would meet the protests of our commercial interests and thus make unnecessary official diplomatic protests. When he sent the proposal of February, 1915, that the English raise the food blockade on Germany if Germany would forego the intensive use of the submarine, he cabled to House:

4. Spring Rice to Chirol, November 3, 1914, Gwynn, ed., *op. cit.*, II, 241.

Please say to Page that he cannot emphasize too much, in presenting the note to Grey, the favorable opinion which would be created in this country if the British Government could see its way clear to adopt the suggestions made there. Opinion here is still decidedly friendly, but a tone of great uneasiness is distinctly audible.[5]

Later in the spring Wilson became more emphatic. He cabled House:

There is something I think ought to be said to Sir Edward Grey, of which I wish you would speak to Page but which I cannot convey through him but must convey through you because I wish it to be absolutely unofficial and spoken merely in personal friendship. A very serious change is coming over public sentiment in this country because of England's delays and many arbitrary interferences in dealing with our neutral cargoes. The country is listening with more and more acquiescence, just because of this unnecessary irritation, to the suggestion of an embargo upon shipments of arms and war-supplies, and if this grows much more before the next session of Congress it may be very difficult if not impossible for me to prevent action to that end.[6]

Three weeks later Wilson wrote:

5. Wilson to House, February 20, 1915, *Amer. Dipl.*, p. 60.
6. Wilson to House, May 5, 1915, Yale House Collection.

The impression prevails here that Sir Edward Grey has not been able to fulfill his assurances given us at the time of the Order in Council that the Order would be carried out in such a way as not to affect our essential rights. There is an accumulating public opinion upon these matters of which I think the Ministers there should know, and the recent explanations do not touch the essence or meet the opinion.[7]

Secretary Lane confirmed Wilson's feeling that Allied interference with American economic rights was arousing opinion to the point where reprisals seemed probable.

I cannot see what England means by her policy of delay and embarrassment and hampering. Her success manifestly depends upon the continuance of the strictest neutrality on our part, and yet she is not willing to let us have the rights of a neutral. . . . If Congress were in session, we would be actively debating an embargo resolution today.[8]

All during the summer of 1915, Wilson pondered the problem presented by Allied methods of trade control. He spoke of it as "this infinitely difficult matter." On July 27, 1915, he wrote: "We cannot long delay ac-

7. Wilson to House, May 23, 1915, *Amer. Dipl.*, p. 68.
8. Lane to House, May 5, 1915, *I.P.*, I, 458–459.

tion. Our public opinion demands it."[9] The reason this prospective action was delayed was the crisis with Germany over the sinking of the *Arabic*. As soon as that was settled, Wilson ordered the preparation of a note of general protest to the Allies in defense of American economic interests. This was couched in strong tones and dispatched on October 21, 1915. It was described by Page as "an uncourteous monster of 35 heads and three appendices . . . not a courteous word, nor a friendly phrase, nor a kindly turn in it, not an allusion even to an old acquaintance, to say nothing of an old friendship."[10] As the winter came on, Wilson's patience with the Allied measures of economic restriction seemed to have reached the point of exhaustion. He daily encountered what he described as the "demand in the Senate for further, immediate, and imperative pressure on England and her Allies." On January 12, 1916, he cabled:

It now looks as if our several difficulties with Germany would be presently adjusted. As soon

9. Wilson to House, July 27, 1915, *Amer. Dipl.*, p. 69.
10. Page to House, November 12, 1915, Hendrick, *op. cit.*, II, 72, 78.

as they are, the demand here, especially from
the Senate, will be imperative that we force England to make at least equal concessions to our
unanswerable claims of right. This is just.[11]

Again the economic dispute was overshad-
owed by the dispute with Germany over
armed merchantmen and the sinking of the
Sussex.

As soon as it was settled Wilson returned
to the Allies.

It seems to me we should really get down to hard
pan. The at least temporary removal of the
acute German question has concentrated attention here on the altogether indefensible course
Great Britain is pursuing with regard to trade
to and from neutral ports and her quite intolerable interception of mails on the high seas carried by neutral ships. . . . The United States
must either make a decided move for peace
(upon a basis that promises to be permanent)
or, if she postpones that must insist to the limit
upon her rights of trade and upon such freedom
of the seas as international law already justifies
her in insisting on as against Great Britain, with
the same plain speaking and firmness that she
has used against Germany.[12]

11. Wilson to House, January 12, 1916, *Amer. Dipl.*, p. 73.
12. Wilson to House, May 16, 1916, *Amer. Dipl.*, p. 74.

This letter was sent at the same time that Bernstorff reported to Berlin that House had told him Wilson could not act against the Allies because of the community of trade interests between America and the Allies. Bernstorff certainly believed what he reported. But there is no evidence in the House papers that the Colonel made the remark. Certainly it did not represent Wilson's belief as indicated in the above letter.

With the extension of the Allied blacklist in the summer of 1916, and the relaxation of the submarine campaign, Wilson approached nearer to the idea of utilizing economic retaliation against the Allies.

I am, I must admit, about at the end of my patience with Great Britain and the Allies. This blacklist business is the last straw. I have told Spring Rice so, and he sees the reasons very clearly. Both he and Jusserand think it is a stupid blunder. I am seriously considering asking Congress to authorize me to prohibit loans and restrict exportations to the Allies. . . . Polk and I are compounding a very sharp note. I may feel obliged to make it as sharp as the one to Germany on the submarine. . . . Can we any longer endure their intolerable course?[13]

13. Wilson to House, July 23, 1916, *Amer. Dipl.*, pp. 76–77.

Wilson thus reached the point of asking for authority to utilize economic pressure against the Allies, which was granted to him by Congress in September, 1916. He did not immediately utilize this authority inasmuch as the presidential election was at hand and he hoped to start peace negotiations between the belligerents as soon as its results were known. That he would have proceeded against the Allies if Germany had not renewed the submarine campaign cannot be assumed. But it is noteworthy that, as we have seen, he wrote to House on November 24, 1916, asking him to pass on to Sir Edward Grey, "in the strongest terms," the dissatisfied feeling of the American people, who were becoming more and more impatient with the situation and whose feeling he believed to be "as hot against Great Britain as it was at first against Germany."[14] It is the more significant in that, precisely at this moment, the Federal Reserve Board issued their warning regarding credits to the Allies. But the whole question of our economic dispute with the Allies was eliminated

14. Wilson to House, November 24, 1916, *Amer. Dipl.*, p. 79.

by the resumption of the German submarine campaign, following the failure of the December peace notes.

Until January, 1917, commercial factors clearly dominated our diplomatic relations with the Allies. Economic interests, however, did not push the United States at any time close to a diplomatic rupture nor even to the point of economic reprisals. Why not? Was our self-restraint the result of counterbalancing economic interests or of political and emotional factors?

The most important factor was certainly the submarine dispute with Germany. Wilson made it plain that he would not press the conflict with the Allies while in the midst of a crisis with Germany; that he would not confuse the issue of property rights and that of human rights. So much he indicated to Bryan in the *Lusitania* crisis.[15] As soon as the *Arabic* crisis was settled, Wilson returned to the Allies with the note of October 21, 1915. Pressure on the Allies was relaxed during the *Sussex* crisis of April, 1916, but resumed after that was settled. Wilson's attitude is illustrated by the beginning of his

15. Bryan and Bryan, *op. cit.*, pp. 406–408, 422–424.

cable of January 12, 1916, referring to the probability of adjustment of difficulties with Germany and insisting that in that case it would only be just to bring pressure on England to make concessions.[16]

Bernstorff always made plain to his government that Wilson would exercise no pressure on the Allies so long as the submarine issue remained unsettled. Throughout the year 1915, he believed that if Germany would renounce the intensive submarine campaign Wilson would act to break the Allied blockade. On July 28, 1915, during the exchange of notes on the *Lusitania* he telegraphed:

He [Wilson] wishes to come to some kind of settlement with us by means of this exchange of notes, in order that he may then turn his attention to England; and his well-known pride confirms him in the view that only after he has concluded his negotiations with us can he take up the matter with her. It should be clearly understood that Mr. Wilson does not want war with us, nor does he wish to side with England, despite all statements to the contrary in the Press of the Eastern States. . . . If we show ourselves ready to help him out of his present difficulties,

16. Wilson to House, January 12, 1916, *Amer. Dipl.*, p. 73.

I am sure he for his part will energetically prose-
cute against England his design of vindicating
the validity of international law.[17]

In his memoirs Bernstorff goes on to argue
that because the German Government could
not decide definitely to give up the submarine campaign, it could expect no advantages from American pressure against the
Allies.

If we had made a clean sweep of it, once and for
all, after the *Lusitania* incident, or, at any rate,
after the sinking of the *Arabic,* as we actually
did after the torpedoing of the *Sussex,* considerable advantages would have been gained from
the diplomatic point of view. To my mind, there
was now only one thing to be done—to abandon
our pretensions that the submarine campaign
was being conducted in accordance with the recognized principles of cruiser warfare, laid down
by international law, and to offer compensation
for the loss of the *Lusitania* and the *Arabic.*
Having done this, we could then proceed to re-
call to the American Government their oft-ex-
pressed original view of the freedom of the seas.
As a matter of fact, immediately after the settlement of the *Arabic* incident, Mr. Lansing sent a
peremptory Note to England. But the prospect

17. Bernstorff to German Foreign Office, July 28, 1915,
Bernstorff, *op. cit.,* pp. 169, 171.

of any favorable result for ourselves from this exchange of Notes was never fulfilled, as our methods of war at sea always resulted in fresh incidents and fresh conflicts.[18]

From the British side, there is the testimony that American pressure against the Allies relaxed the moment a submarine incident took place. Winston Churchill emphasizes the great relief that came to the British in their controversy with America as a result of the first U-boat campaign. Ambassador Spring Rice gave warning after the settlement of the *Arabic* crisis that the British must expect a sharp renewal of the controversy.[19] Colonel House was definite in his opinion of the effect of the submarine campaign:

If Germany had not alienated American sympathies by her mode of warfare, the United States would not have put up with Allied control of American trade on the high seas.[20]

Thus it appears that the chief cause preventing action against the Allies was not of an economic but of a political character: it

18. Bernstorff, *op. cit.*, pp. 175–176.
19. Churchill, *op. cit.*, II, 306; Gwynn, ed., *op. cit.*, II, 282.
20. House to Seymour, June 24, 1933.

was the existence of the sharper conflict with Germany. There were economic factors, however, in the background that militated against bringing economic pressure against the Allies. Assuming that the Germans had finally and completely yielded to Wilson's position on the submarine, could he and would he have acted energetically against the Allies? This is a matter of opinion.

It is certain that Wilson himself believed that it was possible and might be advisable to exercise economic pressure against the Allies. His letters and cables do not raise any arguments of an economic kind *against* such pressure. He does cite frequently the demand *for* it in political circles. On May 5, 1915, referring to this demand, he sent the cable previously cited: "If this grows much more before the next session of Congress it may be very difficult if not impossible to prevent action."[21] On January 12, 1916, he referred to the demand in the Senate "to force England" to make concessions.

Colonel House clearly realized the economic cost of embargoes to the United States. He called Wilson's attention, in the

21. Wilson to House, May 5, 1915, Yale House Collection.

early summer of 1915, to the certainty of a
revolt on the part of "our whole industrial
and agricultural machinery" if embargoes
were imposed.[22] But House, like Wilson, was
affected primarily by the political rather
than the economic factors. He believed that
a serious threat of economic pressure against
the British might be successful, but that the
political cost would be too high.

In regard to our shipping troubles with Great
Britain, I believe that if we press hard enough
they will go to almost any limit rather than
come to the breaking point. But, in so doing, we
would gain their eternal resentment for having
taken advantage of their position, and our action would arise to haunt us—not only at the
peace conference, but for a century to follow.

To this Wilson replied: "I think of it just
as you do," and urged House to make suggestions for "a line of action at once practicable and effective that would escape the
consequences you (and I) would dread and
deplore."[23]

It is questionable whether in the spring of
1916 House told Bernstorff, as the latter re-

22. House to Wilson, July 22, 1915, *I.P.*, II, 58.
23. *Idem;* Wilson to House, July 27, 1915, *Amer. Dipl.*,
p. 51.

ported, that Wilson was no longer in a position to exercise economic pressure upon the Allies because of the community of economic interests between America and the Allies. There is no evidence of this in the unpublished House papers. If the circumstances surrounding the House-Bernstorff conferences of this period are kept in mind, the remark would have no special significance. Both House and Bernstorff hoped to persuade the German Chancellor to accept Wilson's mediation. Bernstorff's whole policy was to get his government to work for a compromise peace. Whereas in the previous year he held out the hope that the Allied blockade might be relaxed under American pressure, in the spring and summer of 1916 he insisted that it was easier to get a compromise peace than any relief from the blockade. Hence he emphasized the difficulties of breaking the blockade. House naturally agreed with him, since he wished to strengthen Bernstorff's efforts for peace.

With these circumstances in mind it is easier to understand the cipher cable sent by Bernstorff to the German Foreign Office, July 13, 1916:

The inactivity of Mr. Wilson [with regard to the Allied blockade] . . . is due in the first place to the fact that no pressure is being put upon him by American public opinion to take action with regard to England. It is obvious that conditions here are not favorable to such action. Those American circles which are suffering financial losses as a result of the English blockade, have no weight in face of the tremendous stream of gold which our enemies have poured lavishly over this country, not haggling over details, and conniving at "graft." For the rest, Mr. Wilson's train of thought with regard to action in respect of England practically coincides with that expressed by Your Excellency. He does not think at present that it is likely to meet with any success, as he has no means of bringing pressure to bear. No one would take him seriously if he threatened England with war. The position is quite different with the President's well-known anxiety to bring about peace in Europe. In this matter he now has the whole of American public opinion behind him.[24]

Bernstorff and other influential Germans later always emphasized the weight of economic factors in leading America to favor the Allies, although it must always be remembered that in the year 1915 Bernstorff's

24. Bernstorff to German Foreign Office, July 13, 1916, Bernstorff, *op. cit.*, p. 279; also in *G.D.*, II, 979.

reports indicated his belief that they would
not prevent Wilson from bringing pressure
to bear on England, if Germany gave up the
submarine. In the eleventh session of the
Reichstag investigating committee, November 14, 1919, Helfferich, who had been German Minister of the Interior, stated:

I take the view announced here by Count Bernstorff, that the business interests were tied up
with England to such an extent that the President either could not or would not interfere to
the contrary effect.[25]

The statement referred to was made by
Bernstorff at the first session of the committee, October 21, 1919. It contains a frequently cited reference to Colonel House:

It was President Wilson's wish that I should negotiate these absolutely confidential questions
continuously with his friend Colonel House, who
lives in New York, and whom I was able to visit
in his home in that city and negotiate with for
months at a time, without its being known in
America, I believe, even up to the present day.
He told me at that time that, as matters had
turned out, Wilson no longer had the power to
compel England to adhere to the principles of in-

25. *G.D.*, II, 724.

ternational law. That the reason for this was that American commerce was so completely tied up with the interests of the Entente that it was impossible for Wilson to disturb those commercial relations without calling forth such a storm of protest on the part of the public that he would not be able to carry out his intention. On the other hand, that Wilson was in a position, and had the power, to bring about a peace without victory; that he had the intention of using this power as soon as the opportunity arose.[26]

Bernstorff's testimony must be read in the light of the fact that he was in a sense on the defense before the investigating committee, attempting to show why he, as Ambassador, had failed to persuade the United States Government to favor Germany. For this reason he emphasized the power of public opinion in America and the factors forming public opinion, among them commercial interests:

Everyone knows that in forming a judgment on American matters, the President alone is not the only one to be taken into consideration. . . . An American President is not at all in the position of accomplishing anything in the face of public opinion. He can influence it, perhaps, and per-

26. *G.D.*, I, 234.

haps stay it, but he cannot accomplish anything against it. In order to form a judgment concerning dealings of the United States, it is essential, first of all, to be absolutely certain as to the condition of public opinion. . . . During the first period, when public opinion in the United States was not neutral, so far as we were concerned, but unfriendly, it was not possible for the government to accomplish certain things. So far as I can judge, generally speaking, the government maintained a neutral standpoint. If my recollection is correct, the legal division of the Foreign Office has always been of the opinion that, formally speaking, the American Government was neutral.[27]

The distinguished German economic expert, Dr. Moritz Bonn, expert for the investigating committee, took the very interesting attitude that while Wilson could not have acted to restrain the Allies in the spring of 1916, because of commercial interests, conditions by the autumn had changed. This he stated to the committee at its thirteenth session, November 17, 1919:

When he [Wilson] stated, in the year 1916, to the Imperial Government, that he could not put an end to the blockade because the interests had

27. *G.D.*, II, 725.

assumed too great dimensions, the fact is that at that time a condition of affairs had developed which he could not venture to challenge. Count Bernstorff has already told us about that. In the autumn of 1916 and at the commencement of 1917, things were quite different. At that time, public opinion in the United States had become much more friendly toward Germany. Press reports of the 12th of December, if I recollect correctly, will be found in the records which deal with this point, which, consequently, do not consist of assumptions or recollections on our part, but of detailed extracts from American journals. Above all, matters had come to such a point at that time that the American population had become bitter about the rise in prices; the harvest had been bad, and people no longer wanted to send great masses of American goods to foreign countries, to the belligerent states. That was one thing.

The second point was that the financial situation of the Allies had become such that they could continue to manage no longer without American credits. This was a fact which Bonar Law, the British Secretary of the Treasury, admitted later quite frankly in the British lower house. The credits given the Allies by the Americans had never been so very great—they were far overestimated here—in comparison with the Allies' needs. . . . The Federal Reserve Board —you knew about this—had already taken steps. At that time Wilson would only have had to have put a restriction upon credits in order to create a deep impression.[28]

The opinion of the German military leaders is expressed in highly emotional terms. Naturally angered by the export of American munitions, they assumed that Wilson's refusal to take forcible issue with the Allied blockade resulted from his pro-Ally sentiments. At the fourteenth session of the committee, November 18, 1919, Ludendorff declared:

The blockade was only possible if the United States agreed to it, and the United States gave its tacit consent, although Wilson had already characterized the blockade as unlawful. . . . So that our unhappy plight bears witness at once to the barbarous conduct of the war by England and the unneutral attitude of the United States. . . . The United States went further in their support of the Entente. I remind you of the shells which were manufactured in the United States, and which bore the American mark of manufacture; and I remember the righteous anger which at that time was bound to flame in every soldier's heart. . . . No soldier believed in the honest neutrality of the United States and of

28. *G.D.*, II, 811.

its President. We instinctively sensed the economic interests which bound up the enormous
fortunes in the United States with England's
conduct of the war.[29]

More realistic and objective in its estimate of the importance of economic factors
in the American diplomatic attitude is the
opinion of the British Ambassador, Sir Cecil
Spring Rice. Like Bernstorff, he was concerned in maintaining the friendliest relations possible between America and the nation he represented. The task was not easy,
since at the time England was stretching
international law. It was his business to tell
his government just how far they could go,
and warn them when they approached the
breaking point. He recognized the value of
the German submarine campaign to the Allies in its alienation of American sympathy
from Germany. He emphasized the importance of the rapidly developing American
trade with the Allies. But he gave warning
that if Allied measures of restriction were
pushed too far, whatever the effects upon
American trade, economic reprisals would
result. His warning of November 3, 1914, re-

29. *G.D.*, II, 857–858.

garding American bitterness against Allied restrictions has already been cited. A year later, following the American note of October 21, 1915, he laid stress upon the favorable diplomatic effects of American trade with the Allies:

The brutal facts are that this country has been saved by the war and our war demand from a great economical crisis; that in normal times Great Britain and her colonies take forty per cent of the total export trade of the United States. We have therefore the claims of their best customer and at the present moment our orders here are absolutely essential to their commercial prosperity.[30]

But in the next autumn he served notice of a change in the attitude of American opinion, coinciding with the estimate of Dr. Bonn. In September, 1916, he reported upon

the hostile disposition of people, generally very friendly, in New York.

I happened to call upon a good friend of ours in the State Department. He burst out in a long and violent diatribe against all our proceedings which he said were doing us more harm than the German had ever done. He surprised me by the

30. Spring Rice to Grey, November 21, 1915, Gwynn, ed., *op. cit.,* II, 300.

extraordinary violence of his language. . . . He was known as being rather violently pro-ally. . . . The case is significant. . . .[31]

The clearest exposition of Spring Rice's opinion is given in a cable to Lord Robert Cecil in the summer of 1916. It reflects the growing irritation of the State Department against the Allied blockade and his own estimate of the importance of economic factors:

The reason why there has been no embargo on arms and ammunition is not sympathy with us, but the sense that the prosperity of the country on which the administration depends for its existence would be imperilled by such a measure. If there is a scarcity of material here, or any other reason why an embargo would pay, we should have an embargo. . . . Restraints on shipping may be ordered. Transport may be impeded. A loan may be made more difficult. We are not secure against such measures. . . . The object should be to ascertain when the breaking point is near and where. There may be a breaking point. Do not deceive yourself as to that.[32]

The frequently cited cablegram of March 5, 1917, from Page is of little historical value

31. Spring Rice to Grey, September 15, 1916, Gwynn, ed., *op. cit.*, II, 349.
32. Spring Rice to Cecil, August 13, 1916, Gwynn, ed., *op. cit.*, II, 345.

in determining the importance of economic factors in American diplomacy. The Ambassador to St. James's was, of all men, in the worst position to judge how far policy in Washington was touched by such factors. He was at the time utilizing all sorts of arguments to induce Wilson to make up his mind to enter the war. Page's reference to a "commercial panic" that would assail the United States if we took no action adds nothing new. It was obvious that if the congestion of American ports, which followed the threat of the submarine, continued, there would be an almost complete business tie-up. Page's telegram would be important only if it could be shown that it affected the decision that Wilson was about to make. All the evidence is to the effect that Wilson made his decision on entirely different grounds.[33]

Surprise has been expressed that there are not frequent references in the American state papers to the economic factors that affected our desire to remain on cordial terms with the Allies. The reason for this is obvious. We were conducting a diplomatic conflict with them over commercial rights. We

33. See *supra,* pp. 82–90.

were laying down as strong a case as possible for damages. Our lawyers naturally emphasized the factors that injured our economic interests and minimized or ignored those that assisted those interests. If the British state papers are studied there will be found constant references to the fact that our economic prosperity was bound up with the continuance of trade with the Allies as well as to the fact that our trade with the European neutrals, even under Allied regulations, was a source of tremendous commercial profit.

It is safe to conclude that so far as Wilson was concerned, there is no evidence that he was deeply affected by economic factors. He evidently strove to eliminate material interests so far as possible from the motivation of his foreign policy. However much Americans were benefiting from commerce with the Allies he was prepared to utilize embargoes, even though the cost were high, in order to secure American rights. But in each crisis the submarine distracted his attention to a more serious attack upon American rights from another quarter. He was quite clear in his own mind that he was in a position to impose embargoes, if such a policy seemed necessary to protect the rights upon which he laid so much emphasis. He never gave any indication that any financial or commercial interests in the United States could bring pressure upon him, the Department of State, or Congress. The only pressure that affected him came from the German submarine.

VI

WILSON AND LANSING

THE Lansing *Memoirs*[1] have received widespread comment as offering indication of the extent to which the American Government during the neutral years, 1914–17, was affected by pro-Ally sentiments and thereby became incapable of maintaining a true neutrality. Mr. Lansing himself makes plain that he believed the future welfare of the United States depended upon Allied victory and that he constantly advocated American intervention in case it became necessary to avert a German triumph. He appreciated clearly the character of Allied infringement of American neutral rights and expressed freely his irritation with Allied methods. But he never wavered in his conviction "that the German Government, cherishing the same ambition of world power which now possesses it . . . must not be permitted to win this war or to break even, though to prevent it this country is forced to take an active part."

1. Robert Lansing, *War Memoirs of Robert Lansing* (New York, Bobbs-Merrill, 1935).

A more significant aspect of the *Memoirs* than this opinion, which was not uncommon at the time, has escaped general comment. This is the convincing evidence they adduce of the resistance of President Wilson to such an argument, and of the fact that Wilson finally brought himself to lead the country into war only because he believed, and was convinced the country believed, that German submarine sinkings of American ships constituted acts of war against the United States. Whatever Lansing himself might feel, whatever might be the color of eastern public opinion as indicated by the press, the President himself controlled foreign affairs and made up his own mind. All through the book Lansing emphasizes Wilson's independence, his tendency "to oppose any action urged by the press or by partizans. . . . The idea of being induced to act under the pressure of popular demand was always distasteful to the President and aroused in him a spirit of resistance."

The major leitmotiv of the book is the conflict of opinion between Lansing, representing the dominant pro-Ally feeling of the eastern seaboard, and the pacifistic Wilson representing more nearly the opinion of the nation as a whole. In each crisis over the submarine it was Lansing who urged strong action against Germany and Wilson who tided it over in the hope of securing peace between the belligerents. The Secretary of State demanded a definite rupture of relations in the spring of 1916, after the sinking of the *Sussex:* "the honor of the United States and the duty of the government to its citizens require firm and decisive action." But Wilson, replying that his impressions were "not quite the same," succeeded in winning from Germany by negotiation at least temporary acceptance of the American contention. Commenting upon the slogan so successfully used in behalf of Wilson in the campaign of 1916, "He kept us out of war," Lansing says: "The value of it was that it was true and everybody knew that it was true." To Lansing's arguments of American interest in Allied victory the President turned a deaf ear. The Secretary of State noted in the autumn of 1916, when disputes with the British were acute:

On no account must we range ourselves even indirectly on the side of Germany, no matter how great the provocation may be. The amazing thing to me is that the President does not see this. . . . For six months I have talked about the struggle between Autocracy and Democracy, and do not see that I have made any great impression.

When Lansing urged the preparation of a decided course of action in view of the probability of the resumption of Germany's submarine campaign, the President did not answer his letters, would not "discuss a policy of action on a hypothesis so at variance with his hope and expectation." Even after the receipt of the fateful note of January 31, 1917, Wilson still hesitated to break relations; said that "if he believed it was for the good of the world for the United States to keep out of the war in the present circumstances, he would be willing to bear all the criticism and abuse which would surely follow our failure to break with Germany."

Wilson's determination to remain at peace was apparently not in the least weakened by Lansing's arguments, for it was as strong in January, 1917, as a year previous. It was certainly not affected by such pro-Ally arguments as those put forward by Ambassador

Page. Quite the contrary. A capital result of Page's conferences with Wilson, according to Lansing, was "to make the President more than ever irritated against the British." Page attempted to arouse the President's feeling against the Germans.

If he had read aright the character of the President, Mr. Page would have avoided taking such a course because it was the one way of arousing Mr. Wilson's spirit of obstinacy. . . . It almost produced a result diametrically opposite to the one which he sought to attain. It was not his insistent demands in favor of the British but the gross misconduct of the Germans, which at last forced the President to break relations with the Imperial Government.

This is the main point of the *Memoirs,* so far as our entrance into the war is concerned. The factor that overcame Wilson's determined pacifism was the German warfare on the seas. But for the submarine, indeed, there was the certainty of a grave diplomatic conflict with the Allies. In discussing British infringements of American neutral rights, Lansing declares:

There is no doubt that the good relations between the United States and Great Britain would have been seriously jeopardized by this unreasonable attitude which seems unworthy of British statesmanship, except for the fact that the British violations of law affected American property while the German violations affected American lives. Nothing else saved our relations with Great Britain from becoming strained to the breaking point.

In the opinion of the Secretary of State it was thus not any pro-Ally propaganda, nor pressure from pro-Ally advisers, nor financial influence, nor any hidden force that brought Wilson to war. The President had given Germany considered warning that the submarine campaign meant a rupture; by his own declaration of the spring of 1916, endorsed by the election of that year, he was thus bound to send Bernstorff home when Germany withdrew her submarine guaranties. Bernstorff himself stated when given his passports: "I am not surprised. My government will not be surprised either. The people in Berlin knew what was bound to happen if they took the action they have taken. There was nothing else left for the United States to do."

Mr. Lansing, although he thus lays our

entrance into the war directly at the door of the submarine, does not consider whether by an embargo upon the export of American munitions it might have been possible to persuade Germany to hold her hand. He makes reasonably plain in his discussion of our diplomatic differences with Great Britain that he did not believe in the principle of surrendering "the legal rights of Americans in order to gain the good will of those who were violating them." The historian, with German sources at his disposal, can show with reasonable certainty that in the winter of 1916–17 the export of American munitions played a relatively unimportant part in leading the Germans to make their fateful decision. The purpose of the submarine campaign was much broader, designed to deprive the British of all vital necessities. Nothing but the prospect of an early peace could have stopped it.

The historical importance of these memoirs lies chiefly in the fact that the contemporary comments express with clarity and force a point of view which members of a younger generation may find difficult to understand, but which was held so widely and in quarters of such influence that it must be accepted as an outstanding historical condition. It is easy to reason, with our advantage of hindsight, that the point of view was irrational; that the welfare of America was no more threatened by a sweeping German victory than by the overwhelming defeat to which we contributed. But leaders of opinion in America from 1915 to 1917 (from which we may exclude any hired manufacturers of opinion) would for the most part have agreed with Mr. Lansing. President Wilson himself, if he could have divorced his official responsibility from his personal sentiment, would conceivably have been one of the number. The amazing thing is the protracted determination with which Wilson for so long refused to be diverted from his loyalty to peace, either by his own emotions or by the opinions about him. Except for the submarine attack, that determination would have been unbreakable.

VII

AMERICAN OPINION ON THE
EVE OF WAR

NOTHING is more difficult to evaluate than public opinion, especially in the United States where there is so much variation from section to section. Equally puzzling is the determination of the factors that form public opinion. Generalizations accordingly are dangerous, not the less so in that they are difficult to refute and if repeated frequently and in simple terms are apt to acquire a traditional sanctity. Such has tended to become the fortune of the generalization that American opinion was brought to favor the Allies by subtle propaganda and the interests of munitions makers and bankers, and that consequently we "drifted" into war with Germany.

That dominant opinion in the East favored the Allies from the start of the war in 1914 has been generally agreed by historians. This bias was clearly discernible before the agencies of either the German or Allied propaganda began to operate. The mere fact of the invasion of Belgium by the Germans exerted tremendous effect upon American opinion. After the close of the war, Ambassador von Bernstorff testified before the Reichstag committee:

Throughout the entire war, the Belgian question was the one which interested Americans most and which was most effective in working up American public opinion against us. Up to the time of the *Lusitania,* there was absolutely nothing else in the entire mass of anti-German propaganda in America, except what bore upon Belgium.[1]

The anti-German bias was sharpened by the progress of events more than it was by propagandist activities. Pro-Ally advocates were strengthened beyond measure by the sinking of the *Lusitania,* the unvarnished story of which prepared the mind of America for a sympathetic reading of the Bryce report upon German atrocities in Belgium. It would have been difficult for British propaganda agencies, which insisted upon sending out the heaviest of reading matter,[2] to have

1. *G.D.,* I, 253–254.
2. See James Duane Squires, *British Propaganda* (Cambridge, Harvard University Press, 1935), pp. 86 ff.

made much progress had it not been for the submarine sinkings.

The further from the eastern seaboard, the less the outrage to feelings by the submarine warfare and the less the enthusiasm for the Allies. British and French sympathizers made little progress in the Middle West and West, and German sympathizers made none in the East. Success of propaganda seemed to depend not upon the skill or activity of the propagandists so much as upon the national penchants and sympathies of the various regional groups. If the pro-German idea had little success in the country as a whole, it was not because pro-Ally interests subsidized news writers, but because opinion did not approve the German idea. So much Ambassador von Bernstorff makes plain in his testimony before the Reichstag investigating committee when asked to explain the failure of German propaganda. There was a difference in basic ideals between the United States and Germany. When it was put to Bernstorff that German propaganda would have been more successful if more stress had been laid upon the purity of German ideals in the war, he replied:

This brings us, of course, to the question of philosophy of life. If, in our propaganda in the United States, we had unqualifiedly found ourselves in agreement with the ideas which governed the American people, then of course we would have been much more successful with our propaganda. But since that was not the case . . . the natural result was that the propaganda fell to the ground.[3]

The reply should be carefully pondered by all students of propaganda in the war. In this case, as in many, it is not so much the seed as the soil that counts.

Whatever the degree and the extent of pro-Ally bias and whatever its cause, American opinion by the close of 1916 by no means inclined toward intervention on the Allied side. America was pacific to the core and Wilson owed his reëlection in November to that pacifism. Secretary Lansing, himself an ardent interventionist, admitted in his *Memoirs* that only German methods of warfare could bring the United States to the help of the Allies.[4] We may remind ourselves of Am-

3. Stenographic Minutes of Reichstag investigating committees, Fifteenth Session, *G.D.*, II, 928.
4. Lansing, *op. cit.*, pp. 18 ff.

bassador von Bernstorff's telegram to the German Foreign Office:

It required the hysterical excitement aroused by the *Lusitania* question, and the incidents connected with it, to produce a state of mind among Americans which at times made war seem inevitable. In the absence of similar incidents, such a state of public feeling could not be aroused.[5]

There was certainly no weakening of this pacific spirit in the autumn of 1916. On the contrary, official relations with the Allies became more acrid. Wilson himself displayed a markedly critical attitude toward the British, and through Colonel House gave warning that American opinion was turning against the Allies.[6]

Concurrently, opinion began to favor Germany as the result of her apparent conduct of submarine warfare according to international maritime custom. This was realized by the Germans. Dr. Moritz Bonn, expert for the Reichstag committee, in his testimony

5. Bernstorff, *op. cit.*, pp. 280–281.
6. Wilson to House, November 24, 1916, *Amer. Dipl.*, p. 79.

laid stress upon the closeness of American
and Allied economic interests in the spring of
1916; but he went on to say: "In the autumn
of 1916 and at the commencement of 1917,
things were quite different. At that time,
public opinion in the United States had
become much more friendly toward Germany."[7] This estimate received support
from Ambassador von Bernstorff, who testified:

The situation in the winter of 1916–17 had become changed . . . since Wilson had been re-
elected on the ground, first, of having maintained peace and, secondly, of having increased
the preparedness of the United States for war.
By the term "preparedness for war," Wilson did
not understand simply an increase of the army,
but the creation of a great fleet, and also, as was
pointed out emphatically in his proclamation,
the creation of a great merchant fleet. Consequently, industries in the United States were
bound to assume that at the moment when peace
was made, activities in industries would get such
an impetus that they could in no way lose as the
result of the conclusion of peace. Therefore, the
feeling in American industries came to be less
hostile to the conception of a peace favorable to
us than it had been before.[8]

7. *G.D.*, II, 811.   8. *G.D.*, I, 278–279.

There was thus no question of "drifting" toward war with Germany. The attitude of the President was fixed: he would prevent intervention unless Germany forced it by the renewal of the submarine attack. He felt himself bound by the result of the election, which he interpreted as emphasizing the determination of America to remain at peace. If there were in existence agencies of pressure for intervention, they did not approach the President.

There are available reports upon the currents of American opinion in November and December, 1916, drafted by the Germans themselves, which are of the utmost historical value. Of these, one in particular may be cited: that of the Counselor of the German Embassy at Washington, Von Haniel, who later became German Under-Secretary of State. His opportunity for observation and assessment of American opinion was unsurpassed. Like Ambassador von Bernstorff, he was objective in his point of view, by no means pro-American but anxious that the German Foreign Office should appreciate the truth of the American situation. The most important of his reports is contained in a let-

ter dated November 10, 1916, sent to Von
Treutler, Minister at German General Head-
quarters. The letter was written at a moment
when the resumption of unrestricted submarine warfare was coming under discussion,
but before any decision had been taken.[9]

Von Haniel emphasized the fact that the
dominant feeling in the United States was
anti-German. He did not ascribe this to economic factors so much as to emotional and
political:

The feeling, above all in high society and in the
press, is, as you know, almost exclusively "pro-
Ally." In view of the close connection with England, from the standpoint of history, blood,
speech, society, finance, culture, etc.—and, in
many of these relations, also with France—this
should cause no particular surprise. And in addition to this there are Belgium, the *Lusitania*,
and the fact that here we are considered respon-
sible for the war, in spite of all proofs to the
contrary. Notwithstanding his commercial instincts, the American is *very* sentimental—often
hysterically so—and in the case referred to,
commercial instinct and sentiment point in the
same direction. . . . Asquith described the one-
sided point of view, and not incorrectly at that,

9. Text of letter in *G.D.*, II, 869–870.

when he said: "Let the neutrals complain about our blockade and other measures taken as much as they may, the fact remains that no neutral national has ever lost his life as the result of it."

Von Haniel's letter continued to emphasize the fact that the determining element in friendly relations between Germany and the United States was the use of the submarine. Except for this issue, America would come to regard Germany with a kindlier eye and might even exercise pressure against the Allies.

Since the "armistice" in the U-boat war, the feeling has quieted down here to an appreciable extent. . . . But as long as it just remains nothing but a simple "armistice," and the sword of Damocles hangs over events in the shape of a recommencement of a ruthless U-boat war, positive and effective work is out of the question. . . . If this danger did not exist, and, moreover, if it were not constantly harped on by Germany, and if unfortunate accidents such as the present case of the *Marina* were not always stirring up public opinion against us, the public, and official circles as well, would present a much more energetic front to the arbitrary acts of the British, which are making themselves felt more and more. Very many American politicians gifted with insight agree upon the point that if the

U-boat question could once be allowed to rest in peace for a moderate length of time—not only from the point of view of actual performance by the avoidance of "mistakes," but also from that of public discussion—the Government would be forced to take steps against England.

Von Haniel went on to raise doubts as to the advisability of a resumption of the un-restricted submarine campaign from the military point of view. He called attention to the fact that it would be necessary, in order to make the blockade effective, to cut off England "completely from all imports"; this he regarded as almost impossible. So long as one way remained open England would hold out, certain that America would come in on account of the ruthless submarine campaign. Above everything, the German Foreign Office must realize that a renewal of that campaign signified American intervention.

There is one point on which we must be absolutely clear. A withdrawal from, or even a material limitation of, the exercise of the so-called concession which we made to the United States this spring in connection with the U-boat war, means war with the United States. . . . This is the absolute conviction of all those here who have paid any attention to the question, and this includes those who were formerly inclined to a different view. No government and no party would venture, without committing political suicide, to give in to Germany on this question, which is one involving the lives of American citizens, after America has so definitely announced what it considers its international rights. The national feeling has risen to such a pitch during the war, and public opinion has become so hysterically sensitive as the result of the continually recurring incidents, exchanges of notes, and proddings by the press, that neither one of them will be able to bear any further burdens of this nature.

Von Haniel insisted repeatedly that the resumption of the submarine campaign would mean an immediate break which inevitably would lead to open war. His remarks were prophetically accurate. War would come not because the American people or government wanted it or sympathized with the Allies, but because the submarine campaign would be regarded as a direct belligerent attack upon America.

A revocation of our promises would be immediately followed by the diplomatic break. Our warnings would not be observed, and the death of an American as the result of a U-boat attack would result in a declaration of war. It is certain that the majority of the people in the country desire to see that peace maintained which gave an impulse to the country which it had never dreamed of, and they are grateful to Wilson because "he kept us out of war." But let the diplomatic breach occur, and the pressure will be too strong. Even the most zealous apostles of peace would not be able to endure the reproach that, by [merely] breaking off diplomatic relations, they had in a sense given Germany a license to kill all Americans in the future. . . . It is equally certain, according to my opinion, that such a war would immediately be carried on by setting in full motion America's endless resources in man-power, money, war industries, ships, etc. Nor are we to expect any effective opposition to be supplied by the German-American element here. They would not be able, nor would they attempt, to bear the brunt of such a national tempest. The days of the *Lusitania* proved this to be the fact.

A telegram from Ambassador von Bernstorff to the Foreign Office, sent two days after this letter of Von Haniel, emphasized the fact that the election of Wilson promised the best chance of peace.

I am still of the opinion that war would have been declared if we had had to deal with a Republican President at the time of the *Lusitania* episode. . . . It is certain that now, when Mr. Wilson owes his re-election to the pacifistic element, he will desire to dwell in peace with us. If on our side we are in the position of refraining from the so-called ruthless U-boat war, the success of which is in any case to the highest extent problematical, I believe that Wilson would do absolutely everything in his power to bring the world war to a rapid conclusion.[10]

A month later, on December 11, Ambassador von Bernstorff drafted a comprehensive report on what he described as "the attitude of American public opinion towards intervention."[11] He began by stating that "The American Press in general takes sides less passionately with either party than was formerly the case, and is heartily tired of the war." He did not believe that this was the result of a development of pro-German feeling. "They don't like us and don't trust us, but have also gradually got to know and not to esteem England." He went on to quote from the *Tribune,* "one of the most inveterate champions of our enemies at the present time":

10. Text of telegram in *G.D.*, II, 1303–1304.
11. Text of Bernstorff report in Bernstorff, *op. cit.*, pp. 332 ff., also in *G.D.*, II, 1029–1042.

"Despite a very widespread sympathy for France and a well-defined affection for Great Britain in a limited circle of Americans, there has been no acceptance of the Allied points of view as to the war, and there is not now the smallest chance that this will be the case. . . . The thing that the British have failed to get before the American people is the belief that the war was one in which the question of humanity and of civilization was uppermost for the British. The Germans have succeeded in making Americans in very great numbers believe that it is purely and simply a war of trade and commerce between the British and the Germans, and the various economic conference proposals have served to emphasize this idea."

Bernstorff emphasized "the consistently friendly attitude of the ten papers of the Hearst syndicate, which come daily into the hands of more than three million readers in all parts of the country." This attitude, he reported, had of late become even much more friendly. "Another factor that has improved the attitude of the American Press towards Germany is the recent important development of the wireless news service, . . . the radiographic transmission of the full reports of American correspondents in

Berlin and on the German fronts to the American newspapers or news agencies." Interesting reports he said had been received "direct and unmutilated" and had "exerted a particularly favorable influence for us."

Bernstorff laid stress upon the desire of the American Government to prevent the newspapers from agitating public opinion in favor of intervention.

It may be particularly emphasized, speaking quite generally, that the great influence exerted by the State Department on the Washington correspondents of the leading newspapers during the last few months, during which there has been a constant threat of the submarine question coming to a head, has always been on the side of peace, with the result that in more than one case, and particularly in the cases of the sinking of the *Marina* and *Arabia,* any serious agitation on the part of the Press has been avoided.

Another aspect of American opinion covered by Bernstorff's report is America's desire that the war should be ended and its conviction that neither side could win a complete victory. "The conviction has for some time been gaining ground . . . that a decisive victory by either of the two belligerent groups of Powers is no longer to be expected." There had been a time when the American press emphasized the economic value of the war to American industry and the suspicion that "Wall Street" would fear the outbreak of peace.

These times, however, are long since past. The desire for a speedy end of the hostilities in Europe is to-day genuine, and shared by almost the whole Press. . . . The general impression left by the utterances of the American Press on the subject of peace is that on the one hand—apart from a small number of influential papers—it is anxious for peace, from which anxiety it is obvious that it intends to pass over the extravagant war aims so often heard from the Entente statesmen; but that on the other hand it cannot as yet find any practicable way of bringing about an early conclusion of peace, and also that it cannot see any advance in this direction in the last statements of Your Excellency, which only a few papers have discussed to any extent.

Bernstorff was as emphatic as Von Haniel in pointing out the impression made on American opinion by German war methods. He called attention to the fact that as soon as

Belgium and the *Lusitania* are mentioned, there are few papers that do not indulge, either in ag-

gressive or more moderate terms, in expressions
of horror at German "frightfulness" and "ruth-
lessness." This deep-rooted feeling of the whole
Press has been once more revived in very re-
grettable fashion by the recent Belgian deportations. The indignation of the Press at this "slav-
ery" which is being imposed on Belgium is general, deep-rooted and genuine. . . . Resolutions
of protest were sent to the President and published in the Press, and indignation meetings on
a large scale are announced to take place in Boston and New York which will offer the Press further opportunities for anti-German demonstra-
tions.

Finally, the Ambassador returned to the
point which he invariably insisted upon, that
peaceful relations between Germany and the
United States depended upon German submarine policy.

With regard to the question of submarine warfare the American Press are quite unanimous on
one point, that a withdrawal of the assurances
given by Germany after the *Sussex* incident, or
even an intentional breach of these, is bound to
bring about, as it were, automatically, a break-
ing-off of diplomatic relations with Germany;
and it is also clear that such a rupture would
only be the first step towards open war. The
great majority of the leading American news-

papers express at every opportunity the genuine hope that such a contingency will not arise.

German testimony as to the depth of America's pacifism, but the intensity of her determination not to submit to submarine attacks, receives support from a source which is free from any suspicion of British influence. Two cables were sent by the *New York American* to its Berlin correspondent, William Bayard Hale, immediately after the dismissal of Ambassador von Bernstorff. Hale was on friendly terms with the Germans and, as expected, handed them over to the Foreign Office. These cables have not received from historians the attention they deserve. The estimate of conditions expressed in them is obviously sincere. Mr. Hearst was anxious that Germany should see the situation as it actually existed in the United States; he did not want America to enter the war to "pull British chestnuts out of the fire." It would be difficult to secure more authoritative judgment on American opinion.[12]

The first cable, dated February 8, 1917, gives warning to Germany that Wilson's ac-

12. Text of the two cables in *G.D.*, II, 1329–1330.

tion in breaking diplomatic relations because of the resumption of the unrestricted submarine warfare, has the national approval:

The sentiment of the American people unitedly supports the President, though many profoundly deplore the necessity for today's action and ardently hope for a restoration of amity. The leaders of Congress of both parties, bankers, even with strong German sympathies, all agree that the President can do no less than protect American lives at any cost. Property losses, however severe, would not justify the rupture of relations. The American press, led by the *Staats-Zeitung,* New York, and the *Staats-Zeitung,* Illinois, will both publish editorials on Sunday supporting the President and hoping that submarines will not wantonly take a single American right, thereby avoiding an open challenge by their dearly beloved Fatherland. The Cincinnati *Volksblatt* is the only German paper in the United States thus failing to support the President, but it says that if war comes, it will be "America first" with every German citizen. The three greatest South American nations, Argentina, Brazil and Chile, according to the press, unanimously support the action of President Wilson, though many condemn the methods of the British blockade. The public here is perfectly calm and there is no hostility shown against Germany. . . . NEW YORK AMERICAN.

The second cable sent to Mr. Hale on the same day gives interesting confirmation of the fact that, so far from drifting toward war with Germany, the American attitude was becoming more friendly at the moment when the unrestricted submarine war was declared. It indicates the feeling that peace could still be secured.

Mr. Hearst urges that a big peace statement from His Imperial Majesty or from Bethmann-Hollweg might solve the whole situation. Americans were getting friendly to Germany and the President was working for the peace which Americans and Germans desired. The German note, especially the two interpolated paragraphs,[13] upset everything; still the President and the country hope for peace. The right word spoken by Germany at this time might completely restore good-will. NEW YORK AMERICAN.

The cables, checking so exactly with the earlier reports of Bernstorff, were bound to prove ineffective. The submarine campaign had already begun and all Germany was by this time agreed that through the throttling of Great Britain peace was to be imposed on

13. Referring to the guaranties offered of safety to one American steamship a week sailing to Falmouth and marked according to German directions.

the Allies. That process inevitably involved the sinking of American ships. American opinion was sober but quite definite in its conclusion that such attacks constituted acts of war.

VIII

CONCLUSION

The principle of utilizing history as a guide to policy is entirely sound, but care must be taken to see that deductions from the past are valid. Easy generalizations are worse than useless. It may well be that we can learn much from our experience of the years 1914–17 that will help us to stay out of future European wars; but we must be chary of assuming that conditions in the future will be at all similar to those of the past. We must be especially suspicious of any simple solution to the problem of neutrality, which by its nature is essentially complex.

It is obviously of importance that we clear the decks by discarding various prevalent impressions of what took us into the last war. Thus it is quite inexact to state that we were drawn in by our export of munitions, which forced the Germans to adopt the method of ruthless submarine warfare. As we have seen, all the evidence available goes to show that even without American export of munitions to the Allies the Germans would have utilized the unrestricted submarine campaign, as the only effective means of striking at Great Britain, which was regarded as the backbone of the Entente Alliance. It is even further from the truth to state that our intervention was determined by pressure from financial groups which had acquired a vast stake in the fortunes of the Allies. Whatever the size of that stake it was largely secured, regardless of Allied victory; it was by no means concentrated in the hands of bankers, but distributed throughout the widely spread groups in America which were strongly pacific. If businessmen or bankers might be supposed to have had an interest in American participation in the war, they had no means of exercising pressure upon the President or upon Congress. We know as a historical fact that no effective pressure was exercised.

Another explanation of our entrance into the war, not so popular for it is not so simple, implies that because of the importance of our war trade with the Allies we put ourselves in a position where we could not exercise effective pressure against them, in the defense of our interests; and that we entered virtually into an economic, if not a political, alliance with them. The argument continues, that Germany could thus justifiably take any measures against that economic alliance, even if such measures injured our neutral rights, and that we merely got what we might have expected. Such a position has elements of far greater apparent historical strength. But it is misleading in that it ignores the point, so frequently made by the German Ambassador, that by injecting the submarine issue at recurringly critical moments from 1915 on, Germany herself made it difficult or impossible for America to meet Allied infractions of commercial rights.

Except for the submarine, our quarrel would have been with the Allies. Upon this Bernstorff, Grey, and Lansing are agreed. In such a case, it is entirely improbable that the diplomatic dispute would have developed into war. Sentimental considerations, economic interests, sympathies of political leaders, all would have combined to produce a peaceful settlement of the quarrel. But all those factors, on the other hand, would have been powerless to drive us into war with Germany if it had not been for the German submarine campaign. There lay the positive cause of American intervention. It is historically isolated, as one isolates a microbe. This can be asserted with confidence, since it is the one cause which if removed would have left us at peace. Without the submarine campaign, we should not have entered the war, whatever other circumstances were operative.

Thus if we ask, "How could we have stayed out of the war?" the first answer must be that we should have had to accept the submarine attacks in a spirit of complete pacifism. We should have had to forbid our citizens and ships the right to travel on the high seas, or else to inform them and shipowners that we would take no retaliatory action if the citizens were drowned or the ships sunk. Because of the practical inability of the submarines to distinguish between belligerent and neutral shipping in the unrestricted warfare, it became in reality an attack upon all shipping indiscriminately. Had we accepted the situation peacefully, the result would have been an effective blockade of American trade and relations, so far as northern Europe was concerned. However pacific the temper of the American people in 1917, it was not prepared to accept such consequences.

We may ask further, could not the Germans have been persuaded to refrain from the submarine campaign by our imposition of embargoes upon munitions? The answer has already been given, that Germany in prosecuting the submarine attack was interested in much more than stopping American exports of ammunition. It is even doubtful whether an absolute embargo upon all contraband, that is, in effect, upon all articles of trade, could have prevented the resumption of the submarine war. Such an embargo would have blighted the prosperity not merely of munitions makers and bankers but of all our industries, small and large, thrown back our laboring classes into unemployment, and ruined the farmers. There would have been so many protests to Congress from the various sections of the country that the maintenance of such restrictions is inconceivable. The great objection, however, to a policy of embargoes as a price to Germany to withhold the submarine, would not have been based on economic grounds. American

opinion would have protested chiefly because it could not approve the surrender, as
Lansing expressed it, of "the legal rights of
Americans in order to gain the good will of
those who were violating them." We may
safely conclude that an embargo upon munitions, in the narrow sense, must have been
futile as a measure designed to avert the submarine campaign, and that a general embargo, for political and economic reasons,
could not have been enforced.

It is obvious that the price of peace, at the
time of the resumption of the submarine
campaign, seemed too high to Americans.
There was no available method by which the
Germans could be prevented from utilizing
the most effective weapon remaining to
them, and America was not willing to accept
submarine attacks without armed retaliation. The circumstances of the next European war may induce conditions similar to,
or quite different from, those of 1914–17.
But it is certain that again a high price must
be paid if the nation is to remain at peace.
Certain restrictions might be accepted by
Americans upon hitherto recognized neutral
rights, such as embargoes upon a carefully

drafted list of munitions or refusal of passports for travelers upon belligerent ships. It must be realized, however, that the moment such restrictions are anything more than a gesture, that is, the moment they become of vital importance to belligerents, they tend to become unacceptable to Americans. Cotton, copper, oil, wheat are quite as important to a belligerent as manufactured ammunition. The practicability of a complete embargo is as questionable for the future as it was impossible in 1916. Furthermore, the experience of the last war showed that our trade with other neutrals may be as important to the belligerents as that with the belligerents themselves. Are we prepared to cut off all our neutral trade?

The policy of legislating automatic embargoes before the outbreak of war or before the character of the crisis can be appreciated, is open to serious objection. Any policy designed to operate automatically in a certain way, under conditions which cannot be exactly foreseen, will break down if conditions develop otherwise than expected. The best example is the embargo upon general loans to belligerents imposed by Mr. Bryan in August, 1914, which in the changed circumstances of the following year could not be maintained. The Department of State was compelled to alter its policy in order to meet the demands of the national interest. An automatic embargo upon ammunition, of the type drafted in the early autumn of 1935, would hardly have caused Germany to pause in her use of the submarine, for it would not have provided for the economic isolation of the British Isles; if it had been extended to all the products which Germany intended to keep out of Great Britain, it could not have been put into successful operation.

Automatic embargoes are apt to prove dangerous as well as futile. They withdraw from the Executive a power which may be of great value in his efforts to preserve peace. The threat of the imposition of an embargo is a powerful diplomatic weapon. Its possession in time of international crisis is worth many battleships. We talk of "throwing our weight" on the side of peace. By surrendering this weapon of diplomacy we automatically lessen the influence which we can exert when war threatens. The right to impose or withhold an embargo, as and when our interests dictate, is one to be jealously guarded, not for the sake of any prestige, but for the value of its diplomatic effectiveness when needed. Any automatic policy deprives us of that right.

The futility and danger of the policy of automatic embargoes applied to "arms, ammunition, or implements of war" has been characterized by a former Secretary of State. Henry L. Stimson writes:

Not only is the President given no power to act in concert with other nations of the world in seeking to prevent a war by putting brakes upon the aggressor who may be starting it, but the action which is provided for may be entirely ineffective in accomplishing its main purpose of keeping us from being embroiled in animosities with other nations.[1]

Americans, almost universally, are intensely anxious to avoid participation in the event of another war. But the nation should not be led into the false hope that we can stay at peace by declaring our isolation, when in fact a European war will touch

1. Henry L. Stimson, "The Illusion of Neutrality," *The Forum*, November, 1935, pp. 261–265.

America, as it did before, in a thousand spots. Peace cannot be legislated through Senate resolutions any more than sobriety could be legislated through Prohibition. The question of peace will depend upon the willingness of the people to accept injuries to American interests without retaliation. Nor should it be forgotten that it is much easier to promise to be patient now than it will be to be patient when the national interest begins to suffer at the hands of belligerents. There is little reason to believe that we, unlike other nations and unlike ourselves in the past, can promise ourselves exemption from the psychosis that seizes peoples in time of war.

The natural conclusion is that the problems of neutrality, under modern conditions, are so complex that there is no practicable method of assurance against implication in another European war once it is started. Legislation designed to isolate us from the rest of the world raises hopes that cannot be fulfilled, for it does not take account of the facts. Those facts are as brutal now as they were twenty years ago. Woodrow Wilson said in 1914, at the outset of the World War:

The occasion is not of our making. We had no part in making it. But it is here. It affects us as directly and palpably almost as if we were participants in the circumstances which gave rise to it. . . . We shall pay the bill, though we did not deliberately incur it.[2]

We can sacrifice certain commercial rights in the hope of avoiding trouble, but experience shows that one sacrifice leads to another, and ultimately we shall reach a point beyond which further concession is impossible. No nation of importance in all history has escaped its problems by refusing to face them.

A definite choice of alternatives is before the United States. If we attempt a policy of isolation, we must be prepared, by developing an armament of such size that it will seriously impress the other nations, forcibly to protect our ultimate vital rights as a nation. Thus only can we create and maintain, for a period, an artificial isolation. Thus only can we prevent a surrender of minor rights from developing into a defense of major rights. Or, we must recognize that the best hope of

2. Wilson to Congress, September 4, 1914, *Congressional Record*, LI, 14738–14739.

staying at peace is to take steps, in coöperation with other States, to prevent war among outside nations which, once started, will surely injure us, whether we are bystander or participant.

The choice of the second alternative must be made if the pacific policy of the nation is to be based upon reasonable and not merely emotional factors. It implies the immediate return to the President of his freedom of action in foreign affairs, of which any policy of "mandatory" embargoes tends to deprive him. Thus we shall revive the spirit of the Constitution, which, as Mr. Stimson points out, left the hands of the Executive very free in such matters, "evidently in a wise appreciation of their complexity and constantly changing character."

Instead of seeking an isolation that cannot be attained, we must emphasize the community of interest that America has with the rest of the world in the maintenance of peace. We ought to negotiate constantly with other States to eliminate the basic causes of war, which can be attacked especially in the economic field. For our own ultimate salvation, we must stand ready to cooperate vigorously with the States whose welfare, like our own, depends upon peace. We must support every measure calculated to stamp out the immediate threat of war whenever it appears.

INDEX

Albert, Heinrich F., Under-Secretary of State, on submarine campaign, 79

Allied blockade, effect on American opinion, 6, 7, 8, 143, 144, 155; methods of, 10, 32, 111; North Sea war zone declaration of Nov. 2, 1914, 32, 58; seizure of foodstuffs designed for Germany, 32, 58; British attitude on proposal to give up blockade if Germany would give up unrestricted submarine campaign and poison gas, 34; effect on Germans, 69, 170; blacklist, 118

Allies, need of American credits, 52, 82–84, 131; need of cargo space, 72 ff.

American opinion, 3, 4, 25, 35, 43, 140, 147 ff., 158, 160, 165

Arabia, sinking of, 161

Arabic, sinking of, 36, 38; effect upon relations with Allies, 116

Armed merchantmen, 39, 63

Austria, sale of munitions to belligerents, 31

Balfour, Arthur J., British Secretary of State for Foreign Affairs, on British need of American credits, 52

Barnes, Harry Elmer, on American financial influences, 85

Belgium, effect of invasion of, upon American opinion, 109, 148, 154, 162; deportations, 163

Bernstorff, Count Johann von, German Ambassador to the United States, on submarine warfare, 17, 18, 21, 23, 35, 50, 90, 121, 122, 151, 163, 170; on peace negotiations, 18, 43, 47; gives notification of final submarine campaign, 22; opinion of Wilson, 23, 47, 51; concedes legality of munitions export, 30–31; on American opinion, 38, 129, 130, 152, 158–164; on *Arabic* crisis, 38–39; warns that submarine warfare will lead to American intervention, 40, 42–43, 44, 49; receives instructions to dismantle German ships, 41; dismissal of, 50, 144; on community of American economic interests with Allies, 118, 127; on Wilson's willingness to break Allied blockade, 121; approves American mediation, 126; on Colonel House, 128; on American neutrality, 130; on effect of invasion of Belgium, 148; on failure of German propaganda, 149, 150; report of Dec. 11, 1916, 159 ff.; on American pacifism, 161; on Allied blockade, 170

Bethmann-Hollweg, Theodor von, German Chancellor, on submarine campaign, 17–18, 21; peace statement of Dec. 12, 1916, 19; desire to maintain peace with America, 41, 46, 47; realization that submarine campaign will lead to American intervention, 49; opposition to submarine warfare, 66

Bonn, Dr. Moritz, economic expert, on American relations with the Allies, 130–131, 151–152

Bryan, William Jennings, United States Secretary of State, surrender of neutral rights, 14; opposition to war, 35; on loans to belligerents, 98–99, 102; breakdown of loan policy, 108, 175

Bryce, Viscount James, report on German atrocities, 148

Churchill, Winston, on German submarine, 7, 123

Clark, Bennett Champ, United States Senator, on export of munitions to the Allies, 56, 78; on economic influences, 106

Congress, United States, pacific attitude of, 3, 54–55

Declaration of London, 111

Embargoes, Wilson's attitude on, 12, 114, 118, 124, 137; proposals for, upon American exports, 79, 110, 114, 116, 118, 119, 135, 172; possibility of, 173; mandatory, 174–176

Falaba, sinking of, by submarine, 34

Federal Reserve Board, warning regarding credits to belligerents, Nov., 1916, 119, 131

Gerard, James W., United States Ambassador to Germany, on German opinion, 37–38, 42

Germany, official attitude toward export of munitions, 30; sale of munitions to belligerents, 31; declaration of Feb. 4, 1915, 31; refusal to give up submarine campaign as offset to Allied food blockade, 34; states that liners will not be torpedoed without warning, 38, 41; peace note of Dec. 12, 1916, 46; attitude of leaders toward American intervention,